DEBT COLLECTION MADE EASY

DEBT
COLLECTION
MADE EASY

Peter Buckland

KOGAN
PAGE

**To better profits
and cash in the bank**

Copyright © Telcrest Ltd 1987

First published in Great Britain in 1987
by Kogan Page Ltd, 120 Pentonville Road,
London N1 9JN
Paperback edition 1988

British Library of Cataloguing in Publication Data

Buckland, Peter
  Debt collection made easy.
  1. Debtor and creditor – Great Britain
  I. Title
  344.106′77   KD1740

  ISBN 1-85091-508-3
  ISBN 1-85091-509-1 Pbk

Printed and bound in Great Britain
by Billing & Sons Limited, Worcester

Contents

Foreword

By Burt Edwards FICM, FIEx, Council Member of the Institute of Credit Management, a Credit Manager for 28 years, author and lecturer.

It is very satisfying professionally to be a part of Peter Buckland's lively new book. His material helps to fill the gap in the UK for readable credit books which are not US orientated or issued by banks or official institutions.

Practising credit managers will recognise the hard-nosed experience which has gone into this book. We have often said, in our hectic jobs, 'If only the sales manager really understood the risk and cost implications or what he is doing', or 'If only the accountant were more commercially aware'. Well, let us do all we can to encourage busy or disinterested managers and staff of all functions to read this book. It is ready to read. Every topic is delivered in alphabetical order on one or two pages. It can be dipped into for essential guidance for enjoyable business reading.

The book is brilliantly clear and full of common sense, but also written in slightly humorous vein. As well as this very readable style, it achieves a remarkable objective—that of making it obvious that credit and collection work is vital not humdrum, and that credit wisdom must be in every manager's business skills, regardless of job title.

The cost job—essentially converting sales efficiently into cash—is without doubt a profit centre in the company. The interest cost of the extra borrowings needed to support slow-paying accounts has a crippling effect on the net profit margin of most companies, large or small. The cost can be ten times as much as a company loses in bad debts, which are individually much more noticeable. A good manager of credit control reduces the interest expense without losing sales. This is why the credit job is a senior commercial one, not an accounting chore for a clerk. Every company should, but many do not, look at its customer portfolio, identify the risky ones, direct sales efforts to liquid, growing outlets, monitor payments and constantly improve the ratio of unpaid sales to total sales. Fewer receivables in relation to volume mean lower borrowings, less expense, faster cash for reuse and more net profit.

Debt Collection Made Easy

This book should rapidly appear on the desk of every person responsible for company profit. It is undoubtedly packed with solutions to all those worrying things we know we don't control properly. This is all delivered with precision and brevity, a rare combination.

Peter's theme throughout is that collection of funds is difficult but vital, and needs dedication, resources and a methodical approach—all born out of a company attitude directed from board level. It is certainly bad news for all those customers who like to play games when it comes to payment time.

I hope that every senior manager and director reads this book. Only then will they be able to reflect on whether they are squeezing maximum profit from sales for their shareholders. The book is great fun to read with a deadly serious message on every page—a rare achievement for a financial textbook.

Introduction

The majority of all trade debts in the UK are overdue. On average, they are overdue by more than twice the agreed period for payment.

This book is designed as a working guide for businessmen and women who have to struggle with the problems of credit control and debt collection.

The debt-collecting techniques are arranged in alphabetical order for quick and easy reference.

You should be able to find and read all I have to say on any topic in less time than it takes to have a cup of coffee—or whatever it is that you have.

Emphasis is on a commonsense approach, with explanations being practical rather than theoretical.

All comments relate to trade rather than consumer credit though many apply to both.

Masculine pronouns are used throughout for convenience only. The information is mostly applicable to women as well, and I do not mean to suggest that all credit controllers or all debtors are men.

The law relates to English law, unless otherwise stated, although most of the techniques have universal application.

The information provided will, if heeded, help you to increase your cash flow, improve your profits, decrease your worries and sleep better at night.

Peter Buckland
London
August 1987

Creditors: A tribe of savages dwelling beyond the financial straits and dreaded for their desolating incursions.

Ambrose Bierce

Aged Debtor Analysis

An aged debtor analysis shows precisely who is causing your cash flow problems, how much of a problem they are causing and how long they have been causing them.

Knowing these facts and acting on them is what credit control is all about.

Here is what an analysis looks like:

Assume:

Terms: Payment of accounts is due no later than the end of the month following the date of invoice.

Date: 1 July (therefore all accounts invoiced in May or earlier are now overdue).

Aged Debtor Analysis

Customer's name	Total debt	Debts not yet due	Debts overdue				Total debts overdue
		Invoiced	Invoiced				
		June not yet due	May under 30 days o/d	April over 30 days o/d	March over 60 days o/d	Before March over 90 days o/d	
Alpha Ltd	£1000	£500	£250	£250			£500
Beta Ltd	£2000			£500	£1000	£500	£2000
Delta Ltd	£3000	£3000					
TOTAL	*£6000	£3500	£250	£750	£1000	£500	£2500
%	100%	58%	4%	13%	17%	8%	42%

*This figure must agree with the total of accounts receivable as shown in your sales ledger.

Application Form for Credit

The amount of information you need on an application form depends on your type of business, the amount of credit involved and various other considerations.

Ideally, most applications for credit would include all or some of the following points and would look something like this:

Application for Credit

1. Full name ....

   ....

   Trading name (if different) ....

2. Legal structure: (a) Sole trader
                     (b) Partnership
                     (c) Incorporated company
                     (d) Other (please supply details)

   ....

3. If an incorporated company:

   Registered address..

   ....

   Registration no ....

   Date of incorporation ....

   If a sole trader: Full name, private address, telephone number

   ....

   ....

   ....

   If a partnership: Full names, private addresses and telephone numbers of all partners..

   ....

   ....

   ....

   ....

4. Trading address and telephone number..

   ....

   Address for invoices and telephone number................................

   ....

5. Names, titles and telephone numbers of those responsible for the payment of accounts ....

   ....

   ....

6. Bankers:

   Name ....

   Address ....

   Account No ....

   Date account was opened ,..

---

7. Maximum credit requirement at any one time
    £ ....

8. Name of managing director or managing partner
    ....

9. Date the business was established ....

10. Three trade references:
    Name, address, telephone number and approximate value of purchases
    during the last year
    (a) ....
    ....
    (b) ....
    ....
    (c) ....

AUTHORISED SIGNATURE ....

NAME (PLEASE PRINT) ....

DATE ....

A signed copy of the form, along with all your terms and conditions of sale which can also be printed on the form, should be given to the applicant.

It is always a good idea to ask for a business card or a letterhead to check off the information there with the information given on the form. This also helps to overcome any problems with difficult handwriting, especially as to the all-important name, address and telephone number.

The most positive men are the most credulous.

Jonathan Swift

Bad Debts–the Real Cost

Bad debts are bad news and even worse than most of us think.

Suppose at the end of a losing struggle you have no option but to write off a bad debt of £1000, and that your administration, financing and collection costs, including solicitors, cost you £200 on the way through.

What is your real loss?

Bad debt written off £1000 plus costs of £200 means a total loss of £1200

The £1200 is miserable enough but consider:

If your normal net profit margin is 10 per cent, you now need to make £12,000 of new sales just to recover your write-off of £1200.

And £12,000 of new sales plus the cost of making those sales without any profit at all really is bad news.

Failure is the opportunity to begin again more intelligently.

Anonymous

Bank References

It is always sensible to know as much as possible about those to whom you intend extending credit. A very good source of financial information for this is your proposed customer's bank.

To obtain their opinion, simply write to them along the following lines:

The Manager
Midlay Bank Limited
44 North Street
London W2 5XP

Dear Sir

Could we please have your confidential opinion on:

    Mr New Customer
    21 Smart Street
    London NW1 8DP

We would like to know if you consider Mr New Customer to be good for trade credit of £1000 per month on 30 day terms.

Also, could you advise us how long Mr New Customer has had his account with your bank.

You may reply to us through our bankers, Natlay Bank Limited, 22 South Street, London SW7 4YA

Yours faithfully

A N Enquirer

For the best results such letters should be as precise as possible as to the amount and terms of the credit proposed.

What you will receive back will be in code. The following may help with the translation:

Debt Collection Made Easy

Code	*Translation*
'Undoubted'	Best reference possible.
'Undoubted for your figure'	Definitely OK for your amount but check again if the credit line is to be increased.
'Considered good for your figure'	Not as good as the above but in the bank's opinion your customer is a good risk for the amount quoted.
'Considered good for your figure. There are charges registered'	Not bad, but the fact that there are charges may be a clue to investigate further.
'Considered good for your account if taken in a series'	Your customer could have trouble paying the stated amount in one go but could probably pay over a period.
'Respectably constituted private company, the directors of which have a long and valued connection with this branch'	Your customer is a reasonable risk for the amount quoted.
'Whilst the transaction of which you speak is higher than usually seen we do not believe the directors would enter into a commitment they were unable to meet'	Good, but the amount involved is higher than the bank considers normal for your customer.
'Respectably constituted company whose working capital is fully employed'	The company is financially stretched. This is a warning to be careful.
'We are unable to speak for your figure'	Cheques are probably being returned and this is a warning not to proceed.

If you still have translation trouble, telephone your own bank manager and ask him for help.

In urgent cases bank references can be obtained by telephoning your bank who will then telephone your prospective customer's bank; naturally, this costs more.

A banker is a fellow who lends his umbrella when the sun is shining and wants it back the minute it begins to rain.

Mark Twain

Bankruptcies

Whereas companies go into liquidation, people go bankrupt or, as the Insolvency Act of 1986 puts it, they become involved in 'personal insolvency'.

A bankruptcy petition can be issued against anyone who has a judgement debt registered against them of £750 or more and who has neither paid that debt nor satisfied the court that there is a valid counterclaim.

A judgement debt is where a debtor has been sued for an unpaid account and the court has found in favour of the creditor and issued judgement against the debtor.

Alternatively, if you are owed £750 or more you may issue and serve a statutory demand on your debtor requesting payment of your debt within 21 days.

If your account is not paid within the three-week period you may then present a petition to the High Court or one of the country's County Courts for your debtor's bankruptcy.

Provided the court is satisfied with your petition it will then make a bankruptcy order against the debtor, placing his assets in the hands of the Official Receiver (a civil servant from the Department of Trade and Industry, known as the OR).

The debtor must submit to the OR a list of all his assets and liabilities.

If considered appropriate by the OR a public examination of the debtor will then be held and creditors can examine him about his financial affairs.

Alternatively, if the OR feels that the debtor has made a full and honest disclosure and that there are no suspicious circumstances, he may dispense with the public examination.

The OR then calls a meeting of creditors to decide whether they will make the debtor bankrupt or let him off by accepting an arrangement for less than 100 per cent of their debts to be paid in full and final settlement.

Often an arrangement is accepted as being faster, more cost-effective and more humane. However, if brankruptcy is decided a trustee will be appointed to sell the debtor's assets and distribute the proceeds among his creditors.

First-time bankrupts are discharged automatically after three years. More habitual bankrupts have to apply to the court after five years and argue their case.

Big Debts — Try to Collect Them First

Many businesses fit into the 80-20 ratio. That is 20 per cent of their customers account for 80 per cent of their debts.

So while it is a good idea to move in on all your slow payers as quickly as possible, it is an even better idea to concentrate your efforts on your biggest accounts first rather than spreading them more thinly and less effectively over all your customers.

Big, slow-paying debts and big bad debts can do a lot more harm to your business than a whole ledger of little ones.

So if you can't give all your accounts equal time and effort start on your biggest one first and work down to your smallest one last.

To know and not to do is not yet knowing.

Anonymous

Big Slow Payers

Dealing with big firms who are also big customers is often a mixed blessing for small businesses.

On the one hand, it is an advantage to have a large volume of business with a minimum risk of non-payment. On the other, it is a disadvantage to have the risk of a large volume of money tied up with a single customer who could be a slow payer.

And there is no doubt that some large companies do have a deliberate policy of delaying payments well beyond the agreed credit terms.

In such cases there is usually not much you can do if you want to trade with them. You either accept their business and their slow paying habits or you don't. The choice is yours.

The vital thing is to know what you are getting into before you get into it and to make sure that, even with the slow payment, it is still a good deal and that you will have enough cash to survive until you are paid.

If you do get caught and the big company's payments department and purchasing manager cannot or will not help then you could try the following approach:

Write personal letters to both the company's chairman and the managing director explaining your position and asking for their help.

For the best results these letters should be marked 'Private and Confidential' both on the envelope and on the letter.

Then if you feel it is appropriate, address them to their homes and send them by registered mail.

For the merchant, even honesty is a financial speculation.
Charles Baudelaire

Bounced Cheques

Section 15 of the 1968 Theft Act says that if you issue a cheque when you know you have no money in your bank you are committing a criminal offence.

The reality is that in most cases it is hard to prove the cheque was issued 'knowingly'.

Nevertheless if you do get a cheque marked 'refer to drawer' or with some similarly depressing comment, immediately let your debtor know what Section 15 has to say.

At the same time also advise him or her that if a cash payment or a banker's draft is not received within the next five days legal action will be the only alternative.

Follow the same procedure with cheques marked 'please re-present'. The only difference here is that any such cheque should be re-presented within the five-day period with a request for an immediate answer as to whether the cheque has been cleared or not.

At the end of the fifth day do not delay. If you haven't been paid, commence action. The chances are that your customer is running out of funds and first in will be first served and maybe even the only one served.

Important

Under no circumstances should a bounced cheque be ever returned to a customer. You may need it as evidence to support your claim.

The shortest answer is doing.

Lord Herbert

Business Failures— The Main Reasons

Businesses fail because they can't pay their bills. The reasons for this are endless but the following are not uncommon.

Lack of capital

Businesses are started with insufficient capital.

Alternatively, there may be sufficient capital but too much of it is tied up in plant, buildings or slow moving or non-moving stock with not enough left over to pay the wages on Friday.

Lack of credit control

Monies owing and due will not pay today's expenses. Also, too many slow payers and bad debts will shrink capital and profits to levels that could make it hard to stay open for more business.

Lack of stock control

Goods which cannot be quickly used or sold but put strains on cash flow.

Similarly, stock shortages delay deliveries, hold up contracts, lose customers and cause money problems.

The trick to stock control is getting the balance right.

Lack of experience

Insufficient knowledge or experience of an industry or of business generally (ie breakeven points, profit margins, cash flow, VAT, tax, PAYE etc) can quickly bring on the end.

Lack of retained profits

The ploughback of profits for replacement of fixed assets, carrying more debtors, increased stock requirements or more working capital, is basic to almost every business.

Net profits of £30,000 with directors' drawings of £25,000 will not generally help a business—except to collapse.

Overtrading

Businesses rarely stand still. The direction is either up or down, with up being preferable.

Before expanding, arrangements must be made for the higher cash requirements needed to support trading at increased levels. If not, the risk is of expanding to bust.

Customers or suppliers failing

A high percentage of businesses fail because of the collapse of a major customer or a specialist supplier.

It is imperative to watch and be aware of these areas of vulnerability.

Staff changes

So often the loss of a key executive who possesses certain skills and abilities is the beginning of the end.

The easiest way to make money is to stop losing it.

Cash Flow

This is the money that comes in and goes out of your bank account.

If you are going to stay in business it is important that more comes in than goes out.

To know if this is happening and is likely to continue, use a cash flow chart.

Cash in comes from your deposit book and cash out comes from your cheque book. The only other items you need to record are debits or credits made directly by the bank to your account.

The opening bank balance is that shown on your statement at the close of business of the day before the chart begins. It needs to be adjusted for any unpresented cheques or unrecorded deposits.

For maximum benefits from the chart be conservative about your income budget forecast and the opposite about your payments forecast.

Your job isn't making things or providing services. It's making money.
Anonymous

24

Cash flow chart for period _____ to _____

ENTER PERIOD (eg weekly, monthly or quarterly)

RECEIPTS	BUDGET	ACTUAL	BUDGET	ACTUAL	BUDGET	ACTUAL	BUDGET	ACTUAL	BUDGET	ACTUAL
SALES INCOME										
Cash Sales										
Payments from Debtors										
CAPITAL INCOME										
Loans										
New Capital										
Sale of Assets										
OTHER INCOME										
Commissions										
Investment Income										
Rent										
VAT										
SUNDRIES										
Specify 1										
2										
3										
4										
TOTAL RECEIPTS										

RECEIPTS

25

PAYMENTS

TRADING EXPENSES

Cash Purchases

Payments to Trade Creditors

Wages (including NHI)

ADMINSTRATION & SALES EXPENSES

Advertising

Carriage and Packing

Directors' Remuneration (including NHI)

Entertaining & Travelling

General Expenses

Heat, Light & Power

Hire & Leasing Costs

Interest Charges—Bank Charges

Insurance

Legal, Audit & Professional Fees

Motor Vehicle Expenses

Postage & Telephone

Printing & Stationery

Rent & Rates

Repairs & Renewals

PAYMENTS

Salaries (including NHI)										
Sales Commissions & Expenses										
CAPITAL EXPENSES										
Capital Purchases										
HP Payments (including interest)										
Loans										
OTHER PAYMENTS										
Corporation Tax										
Dividends										
VAT										
SUNDRIES										
Specify 1										
2										
3										
4										
TOTAL PAYMENTS										
DIFFERENCE BETWEEN										
RECEIPTS & PAYMENTS (+or-)										
OPENING BANK BALANCE (+or-)										
CLOSING BANK BALANCE (+or-)										

Certified Cheques and Bankers' Drafts

If you need to be absolutely sure that you really do have your money in your hand and not just a piece of paper which may or may not be paid, ask for one or other of the above.

A certified cheque is an ordinary cheque which has been certified in writing by a bank as being good. Such cheques will bear the bank's stamp and a bank official's signature on their face.

Similarly, safe cheques are those issued directly by the established banks themselves. Such cheques are known as bankers' drafts.

Both are as good as money in the bank.

He that resolves to deal with none but honest men must leave off dealing.

Proverb

Collecting by Contra

When two businesses are both buying from and selling to one another the outstanding accounts between them can be offset and the net balance paid by whoever owes it to the other. This is settlement by contra.

It is best in such cases to set out the contra agreement in writing right at the outset. This will help to avoid any misunderstandings or arguments as to when, how and what will be settled by contra.

Collecting by contra is not allowed if your debtor becomes insolvent unless there is a prior established pattern of setoff. In such cases a written agreement can strengthen your case and perhaps save you some money.

From an administration point of view contra is generally a messy form of collection, especially when VAT is involved. It is not recommended unless you have worries about collecting in the more usual ways.

There is no security on this earth, there is only opportunity.
Douglas MacArthur

Collecting by Letter

A collection letter has only one purpose—to collect your money in the shortest possible time.

To maximise your chances of this:

Be clear

Write as you would speak. Don't use long words or flowery sentences. Don't beat about the bush. Just ask for your account to be paid and for it to be paid quickly.

Be specific

Tell your debtor precisely how much to send, where to send it, when to send it and what it covers.

Also explain what will happen if he doesn't send it.

Be courteous

A polite but firm approach gets better results than a rude but firm approach. Also, you may want to do future business so look after your trading goodwill.

Never apologise for writing and asking for your money. It is your overdue customer who should be apologetic.

Be sensible

Don't ask for payment in full or part payment because there are no prizes for guessing which one you'll get.

Don't ask why a debt hasn't been paid because you'll get what you asked for . . . an excuse and not necessarily your money.

Be credible

Never threaten any action that it is not your real intention to carry out.

If you say you are going to do something and you don't, you will not only lose credibility, impact and effectiveness but also give your debtor further confidence to continue not paying.

Be urgent

Your letter should have a feeling of 'action required today'. It should not give the impression that tomorrow, next Monday or the end of the month is soon enough. You want to be paid now, today.

Be reasoned

Give your debtor a better reason for paying his account than for not paying it, such as:

1. He will protect his credit reputation
2. He will be able to trade with you again
3. He will avoid having to pay cash in the future
4. He will avoid third party involvement
5. He will avoid legal action
6. He will have done the right thing.

Be personal

Avoid the faceless approach and write to a named executive who has authority to approve the account for payment; have the letter signed by the person whose printed name and title appears as the sender of the letter.

Letters should appear to have been typed individually.

Don'ts

1. Don't use pre-printed form letters where you just fill in the gaps for date, name, address and amount.
2. Don't fail to mention previous letters you have written and which haven't been answered.
3. Don't label letters 'first reminder' and so on, as you are telling your debtor there are still plenty to come and there is no need to hurry with his payment.
4. Don't write to individual debtors if historically letters have had no effect on them but other methods of collection do.

Debt Collection Made Easy

5. Don't write more than two letters. The law of diminishing returns applies.
6. Don't write the same letters month after month and year after year. Vary them so that your customers don't get used to your routine.

Sample first letter

14 November 19XX

Dear Mr Slowpayer

Invoice No A109 for timber frames
dated 18.09.XX for £223.41

As you know from the invoice and our subsequent October statement your above account is now overdue.

To rectify this please mail your cheque for £223.41 to reach us at the above address no later than the 21st of this month.

By doing this you will protect your credit reputation with us and will avoid having to pay cash for any future purchases.

A pre-addressed envelope is provided for your convenience.

Please attend to this matter now and put your cheque in today's post.

Yours sincerely

Les Hardy
Credit Manager

Sample final letter

21 November 19XX

Dear Mr Slowpayer

Invoice No A109 for timber frames
dated 18.09.XX for £223.41

I wrote to you on 14 November requesting payment of the above account. To date I have received no reply to my letter nor has the account been paid.

In view of this I have little option but to inform you that unless we receive payment of the £223.41 within 72 hours of today's date we shall refer the matter to a third party to take whatever action they consider appropriate.

I trust this will not be necessary, but unless payment is on my desk by noon of 24 November you leave me no alternative but to proceed.

Yours sincerely

Les Hardy
Credit Manager

Sample final letter (stronger)

---

21 November 19XX

Dear Mr Slowpayer

Invoice No A109 for timber frames
dated 18.09.XX for £223.41

I have received no reply to my letter to you dated 14 November requesting payment of the above account.

In view of this we have now had a County Court summons drawn up in your name for the outstanding balance plus our costs plus interest.

As you can see from the photostat enclosed this summons is dated 26 November and unless we receive the £223.41 by noon on that day the summons will be automatically served on you.

I trust this will not be necessary.

Yours sincerely

Les Hardy
Credit Manager

NOTE: Enclosed with the letter will be an actual copy of the summons to be issued.

Sample letter (dishonoured cheque)

14 November 19XX

Dear Mr Slowpayer

Invoice No A109 for timber frames
dated 18.09.XX for £223.41

Your cheque in settlement of the above invoice has today been returned to us marked 'refer to drawer'.

As you may know, the Theft Act 1968 says that if you issue a cheque when you know you have no money in your bank, you are committing a *criminal offence*.

In view of this, I strongly recommend you protect your position by settling this matter by means of cash payment or a bankers' draft, to be received by us no later than noon on Thursday 19 November.

If this is not done, the matter will be necessarily and automatically referred for immediate legal action.

Yours sincerely

Les Hardy
Credit Manager

His style is chaos illuminated by flashes of lightning.
As a writer he has mastered everything except language.

Oscar Wilde

Collecting by Telephone

Try collecting by letter first. It is cheaper than telephoning and a lot of the time it works. When it doesn't, start dialling.

The advantage of the telephone is that it is a two-way communication which gives you the chance to assess at first hand (or ear) why your account is not being paid.

Is it because of:

(a)   A query or dispute?
(b)   A money problem?
(c)   An oversight?
(d)   A deliberate policy?
(e)   Something else?

Once you know or can guess the reason, and this should be obvious from your conversation, you can decide what action to take.

Telephone techniques

Before dialling make sure you know:

1.   Your debtor's correct name and legal status
2.   Who you need to talk to to get the account paid
3.   The amount, date and full details of the debt
4.   The agreed terms and conditions of sale
5.   Details of any previous communications about the debt
6.   Date of last payment received
7.   Debtor's previous payment record
8.   How you are going to respond to excuses or requests for time extensions or part payments.

The golden rules are to be polite, persistent and to personalise the conversation as much as possible. Give your name and call him by his—make it him and you. Be interested and listen to what he says, and make notes of the conversation for future reference.

Before hanging up, make sure you have a firm commitment from your debtor to take a definite action by a definite date.

If that action is not taken within the agreed time and your debtor's promise is broken you must immediately move to the next collection stage. Do not dither or offer second chances.

If you continually cannot get through to your debtor, the message is as clear as if you had spoken to him. Don't delay and hope. Move on to the next stage.

If your debtor tells you your cheque is in the mail ask the following questions:

When was the cheque sent?
Where was the cheque sent from?
What is the date and number of the cheque?
What is the amount of the cheque?
If it is not for the full amount of the debt, why isn't it?

If your debtor agrees that your cheque will be ready on a definite future date and it's practical, say, 'Fine. I'll come down on that day and pick it up from you at 2pm. Please make sure it's ready at reception.'

This will help to sort out the genuine cases.

If it's not practical to visit your debtor and he has promised a cheque for a definite future date try, 'Fine. Put the cheque in the mail today with that date on it and I'll hold it until then before banking it.'

Again, this will add a touch of reality to the situation.

Tips

Telephone collecting is not cheap. Make sure you are being cost-effective, particularly with smaller accounts.

Phone as much as possible, especially for the long distance calls, during the cheaper telephone period after 1pm.

The more you do of what you've done the more you'll have of what you've got.

Anonymous

Collecting by Telex

If you and your debtor both have Telex it is well worth using.

- It is fast.
- It creates a written record which your debtor cannot deny receiving.
- It carries a sense of urgency.
- It is still unusual enough to attract attention.
- It arrives at a different time from the rest of the mail.
- It does not come in an envelope and it could be seen by anyone in the office which may, in itself, help to achieve its purpose.

Similar comments apply to collecting by facsimile machine (fax) or by using telemessages.

Success seems to be largely a matter of hanging on after others have let go.
William Feather

Collecting in Person

Despite the time and inconvenience involved, this is the most effective method of collection.

It is also the most expensive, the least popular and the most rarely used.

The advantage is that your debtor has either to pay you or not pay you; if the latter, you have saved time in assessing the situation and can immediately get on with whatever action is necessary.

If your debtor won't see you or is not available whenever you call, you can draw your own conclusions and similarly get on with the necessary action.

For the purposes of future collections or for legal proceedings always make notes of what happened and what was said. They may come in handy.

Many a man's tongue broke his nose.

Seamus MacManus

Compositions

Not the story type, although a story is always involved.

This type of composition is when some or all of the creditors of a business in trouble agree to accept less than 100 per cent of their outstanding debts in full and final settlement of their claims.

The advantages of this arrangement are that the formalities and costs of insolvency are avoided and settlement can be made quickly and with minimum fuss.

For a composition to work it must be agreed to by a majority of creditors both in numbers and in value.

When property is assigned to a trustee for dividing among the creditors as part of the composition, this is called a *deed of arrangement*.

If you trust too much you may be occasionallly deceived. However, you will live in torment if you cannot trust enough.

Anonymous

Computers in Credit

Computers are fast adding machines that can store information.

Most people involved with them belong to a cult that speaks a language few of us understand. I suspect this is so that we can't talk back or properly assess their charges or claims.

Nevertheless computers are a great help with credit management in preparing invoices, statements, follow-up letters and a wide range of analysis reports.

For best results from your computer:

1. Don't change from a manual system to a computerised one over the weekend. Although a bit of a nuisance, it is usually cheaper and safer in the long run to run both systems together until you are 101 per cent sure that your new computer is ready and able to handle what you want it to.

2. Be sure that you are happy and satisfied with your manual system before computerising it.

3. Only order the program you need, not what would be nice to have. It is very easy to end up wasting a lot of time and money preparing reports that you don't read and no one else does either.

4. Be clear and precise when explaining what you want your computer to do. Programs are expensive, and even more so if you have to keep altering them.

    It is much cheaper to spend a little longer thinking about them beforehand and getting them right the first time rather than the second, third or fourth time around.

There is no expedient to which man will not resort to avoid the real labour of thinking.

Sir Joshua Reynolds

Consignment Accounts

This is a handy tool if you have reservations about a customer's financial ability but you still want to do business with him.

Instead of selling him your goods, you let him have them on consignment.

This means he gets physical possession of the goods but you keep their legal title.

Your customer then pays you for what he sells. If he doesn't, or if he doesn't sell anything, you simply call around and take your unsold goods home—that is provided you can find them.

The documentation for this type of arrangement should be drawn up by a solicitor experienced in such matters.

Frustration is not having anyone to blame but yourself.

Anonymous

Credit Cards

If you can't or don't want to give credit yourself and your business should give credit you may be able to solve the problem by using the money of one or more of the credit card companies instead of your own.

Your customers will be happy because they will get the credit they want.

The credit card companies will be happy because they'll have more business.

And you should be happy because you have made your sale, given your customers credit, and avoided giving it yourself.

The only drawback is the 1 to 6 per cent of sales value that you will have to pay for having this service available to you.

So, depending on whether you are in the type of business that suits credit cards and whether your profit margins can stand it, plastics may be an answer for you.

Plastics: Group of synthetic resinous or other substances that can be moulded into any form.

The Concise Oxford Dictionary

Credit Insurance

If the future of your business could be put in jeopardy by one or two of your main customers not being able to pay you, credit insurance may be worth consideration.

However, if your customers are well spread and the write-off of a couple of the larger ones wouldn't cause too much trouble then credit insurance may not be commercially viable for you.

The cost varies with what you want covered, the risks involved, your credit management history, and other relevant factors. However, as a broad generalisation, premiums are usually around 0.5 per cent and upwards of the annual sales you want covered.

Also, the insurers will not necessarily cover all your customers and those that they do cover may only be covered up to a certain amount.

The insurer's decision on whether to provide cover, and if so how much, depends on what the insurer thinks of you and your customers' credit ratings.

You should also know about claims. If your customer becomes insolvent or for some other claimable reason doesn't pay, what your insurance company settles with you when you claim is not 100 per cent of your loss but usually more like 80 per cent—the balance of the loss is still yours. And that's not even necessarily 80 per cent of the total loss. That's 80 per cent of the agreed cover.

Also, disputed accounts are normally not eligible for claims until the disputes are resolved.

Finally comes settlement, but don't count on this to pay your accounts at the end of the month. Settlement can be a drawn out affair and can take as long as six months or more from the time your debt became overdue.

Insurance. An ingenious modern game of chance in which the player is permitted to enjoy the comfortable conviction that he is beating the man who keeps the table.

Ambrose Bierce

Credit Limits

Having decided to extend credit to a new customer you should:

1. Create a file containing the application form, bank references, status reports and any other applicable notes or documents.
2. Decide on a credit limit and a date for its review. This should be based on your customer's requirements and your assessment of his ability to pay.
3. Mark the limit on the customer's account in the sales ledger and make sure that whoever is involved in sales or in order taking knows what it is.
4. Review the limit on a set date in the light of your experience and any new information received. But also review the limit on an ongoing basis if you have any doubts.

If a request is made to exceed the limit a conscious decision needs to be made. However, the very fact of having a limit will at least draw your attention to the situation and the need for re-assessment.

The man who insists on seeing with perfect clearness before he decides, never decides.
Henri Frederic Amiel

Death Rate

About half the companies set up in the UK over the last 10 years are no longer with us.

And a high percentage of these companies died before their second or third birthday.

The reason for a lot of these premature deaths was that their owners did not sufficiently understand the importance of cash flow.

Maybe in the national interest new company incorporation certificates should carry an official government warning!

> BEWARE! LACK OF CASH FLOW CAN SERIOUSLY DAMAGE YOUR COMPANY'S FINANCIAL HEALTH.

Even in the shadow of death, two and two do not make six.

Leo Tolstoy

Debt Collectors

Debt collectors do it better because if they don't get your money and look after your goodwill they don't get paid and if they don't get paid they are not around very long.

Also, they do it better because they have an advantage you don't—another name.

Debt collectors are a third party and that point alone often has enough psychological impact to get a debtor to pay them on their very first approach.

Your debtor doesn't mind you knowing he is a slow payer but he doesn't want a professional third party to know. The risk that this information might become generally available and affect his future ability to get credit is too great.

The debt collector's other advantage is that he has no other job. He has none of the other worries or tasks that you have to deal with daily. His only job is to get your money and he will do this by tried and proven methods of systematic and persistent follow-up.

But do they hurt your image?

If you let your debtors get away with not paying or late paying you are only hurting your own image by letting it be known that your credit control is open to abuse and that you can be financially pushed around.

By reinforcing your credit policy a reputable debt collector can not only recover your monies but can also let your customers know that you run an efficient business and that you expect them to do the same by paying you as and when agreed.

Warning

Before signing on with an agency:

1. Check that they are registered with the Office of Fair Trading.
2. Get a banker's reference on them.
3. Talk to some of their other customers.
4. Make sure that you are fully aware of their terms and conditions of trade.

There are but two ways of paying a debt—increase of industry in raising income, increase of thrift in laying it out.

Thomas Carlyle

Discounts

In most cases it is better to improve your credit control than to give a discount to entice payment.

The reasons for this are:

1. It can play havoc with your bookkeeping and create chaos with your VAT.

    It means your statements or invoices must show both the lesser amount due with VAT if the discount is taken, as well as the amount due with VAT if the discount is not taken.
2. It often results in late payments with the discount still being taken. This in turn can lead to disputes.
3. It can give away too much profit. If your net margin on sales is 10 per cent and the discount offered for early payment is 2.5 per cent, you are effectively giving away a quarter of your profit.
4. It is expensive. Giving a 2.5 per cent discount to get your money in 30 days instead of 60 means that your money is costing you 2.5 per cent for 30 days. That's 2.5 per cent per month, or 30 per cent per annum. That's expensive.

However, if you do want to give an incentive for early payments, consider a settlement rebate. This is where you agree to a percentage rebate on sales at the end of each year, half year or quarter. The rebate is usually conditional on your accounts being paid on time and a certain sales value being exceeded. It can, of course, be based on whatever criteria you want.

When it is a question of money, everybody is of the same religion.

Voltaire

Excuses

Anyone trying to get their accounts paid will have heard these ad nauseam:

We have lost your invoice.
We don't have a statement.
We haven't done a reconciliation yet.
We didn't receive the goods.
We didn't order the goods.
The goods were delivered to the wrong place.
The goods delivered were the wrong ones.
The goods delivered were damaged.
The goods were delivered too late.
The cheque signatory is away.
Our computer has broken down.
All our accounts are with the auditor.
It is our stocktake and everyone is busy.
We pay all our accounts at the end of the month.
Our accounts department is being moved.
The company has been taken over and all payments are suspended.
We are going into liquidation.
The VAT man is in and we can't get our accounts.
Your statement didn't show our last payment.

and yes, that old favourite:

IT'S IN THE POST.

The only way to handle excuses is to treat them for what they are and get on with the business of collecting your money.

'One can't believe impossible things.'
'I daresay you haven't had much practice,' said the Queen.
'When I was your age, I always did it for half-an-hour a day. Why sometimes I've believed as many as six impossible things before breakfast.'
Lewis Carroll

Factoring

Up to 80 per cent of your credit sales can be immediately turned into cash by the simple process of factoring.

All you have to do is send the invoices you want factored to your factor and, provided they approve the accounts they will send you a cheque for around 80 per cent of their value by return mail.

They will then send out statements in their own name and your customers will pay them instead of you. When they collect you will get the 20 per cent or so balance still owing. However, if they don't collect you may have to pay back the 80 per cent you have already received.

The costs of factoring are usually around 0.5 to 3 per cent of your turnover plus an interest rate roughly equivalent to your bank overdraft rate, so unless you have reasonably high profit margins costs can be a problem.

The pluses are that you speed up your cash flow, and the majority of your sales administration and collection work is done for you.

On the minus side is the fact that a lot of your customers won't like dealing with and paying a factor. Also, there is often the suspicion that there is something wrong with a business that has to use factoring to raise money. However, as the industry grows factoring is becoming better understood and this attitude is gradually changing.

Everyone in Vanity Fair must have remarked how well those live who are comfortably and thoroughly in debt: how they deny themselves nothing: how jolly and easy they are in their mind.

W M Thackeray

Financing Debtors

If your sales average is £50,000 per month and all your customers pay you precisely one month after the sale date, at any one time your outstanding debtors will average £50,000 or 8.3 per cent of your annual turnover.

If your customers pay you in two months your average monthly debtors outstanding will be £100,000 or 16.7 per cent of your annual turnover.

If they take three months you will be financing 25 per cent of your year's sales and at four months you will be financing 33.3 per cent.

In money terms the annual interest cost to you of providing credit to your customers is calculated by taking the value of your average monthly debtors outstanding and multiplying the figure by the current overdraft rate.

This figure does not, of course, take account of what you could earn on or do with your money if it was available to you.

Yearly interest cost of financing debtors

Average monthly value of debtors	Interest cost at				
	5%	10%	12.5%	15%	20%
£10,000	£500	£1,000	£1,250	£1,500	£2,000
£20,000	£1,000	£2,000	£2,500	£3,000	£4,000
£30,000	£1,500	£3,000	£3,750	£4,500	£6,000
£40,000	£2,000	£4,000	£5,000	£6,000	£8,000
£50,000	£2,500	£5,000	£6,250	£7,500	£10,000
£100,000	£5,000	£10,000	£12,500	£15,000	£20,000
£500,000	£25,000	£50,000	£62,500	£75,000	£100,000
£1000,000	£50,000	£100,000	£125,000	£150,000	£200,000

Note. If your net profit on sales is 5 per cent and your interest costs are 10 per cent, your entire profit will be lost if you are not paid within six months.

If your interest costs are 15 per cent your profit will be lost after four months of non-payment.

Five Types of Customer

There are five standard types of customer:

1. Prospective customer
2. Customer
3. Slow paying customer
4. Bad debtor
5. Write-off

The following graph gives a general idea of how quickly the real value of those customers' accounts erode if they are not collected and slip down the scale to customer 5.

The increasing loss to you reflects the expenses involved in administration and collection, the loss of use of your money, the effects of inflation and interest and finally, the cost of bad debt write-offs.

Increasing loss of value of overdue accounts

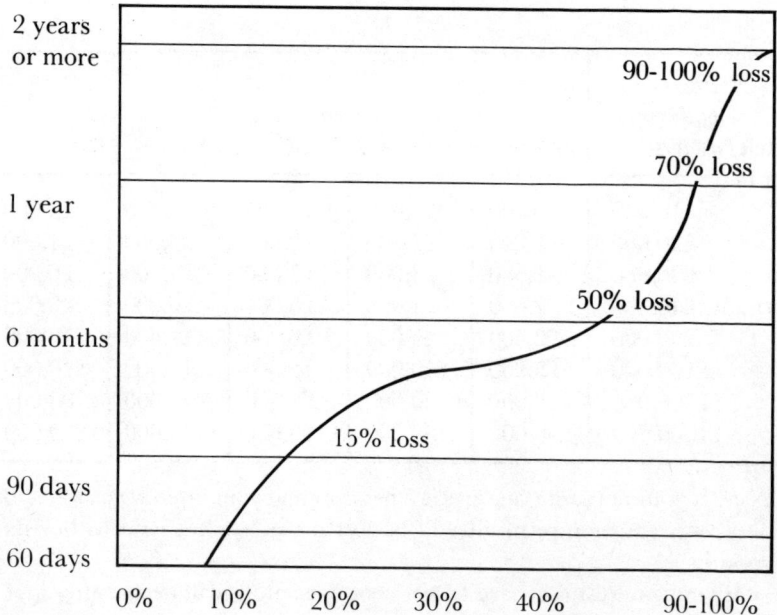

We forge the chains that bind us.

Charles Dickens

Follow-up Procedures

These depend on your business's requirements, your personality and your relationship with your customers.

However, the best way to keep yourself in cheques and your customers in check is to have a follow-up plan and to work that plan.

The following plan will work for most businesses:

Action	Timing
Invoice	As soon as possible
Statement	Same time each month
Reminder letter	Maximum 14 days after account becomes overdue
Telephone follow-up	Maximum 7 days after reminder letter
Final notice	Maximum 7 days after telephone follow-up
Referral to a third party or to litigation	Maximum 7 days after final notice

Use a 7- or 14-day interval between actions. That way your follow-up is always on the same day of the week and is easier to remember and organise.

Periodic purges are no good. For any plan to be effective it must be precise, organised, systematic and worked.

Important

Allow for preferential customers.
Allow for well established and acceptable payment patterns.
Vary your cycle from time to time to maintain impact.
Watch for changing payment habits.
Know what stage you are at and what will happen next and when.

Good Collecting–What it Means

Suppose:

Your sales average £100,000 per month (£1.2 million per year).
Your overdraft rate is 14 per cent.
Your net profit is 5 per cent on sales.
Your average accounts receivable at any one time are £216,000 which means they are outstanding for an average of 67 days.

Suppose:

That through good collecting your average accounts receivable are reduced to £150,000, which means they are outstanding for an average of 45 days.

The result is:

1. Your overdraft will now be £66,000 less (£216,000 less £150,000).
2. Your interest on your overdraft will be £9,240 less per annum (14 per cent of £66,000).
3. Your net profit will increase from £60,000 (5 per cent of £1.2 million) to £69,240 (£60,000 plus the interest saved of £9,240).
4. Your net profit sales will increase from 5 to 5.77 per cent (ie £69,240 on £1.2 million).

That's what it means.

Goals are as essential to success as air is to life.

David Schwartz

Governments, Councils and Local Authorities

There is little risk here. That is, little risk that you will be paid on time. All are well established and notorious slow payers.

When dealing with them, all you can do is ask if there is any method by which their payout system can be speeded up, such as by presenting your accounts in some special way or whatever.

If there isn't, ask what is a realistic period in which you can expect your accounts to be paid, add a margin of 50 per cent and allow for this in your profit margins and liquidity levels.

The authorities were at their wits' end, nor had it taken them long to get there.
Desmond Macarthy

Guarantees

A guarantee is a promise by a third party which, if properly drawn up, will make that party legally liable to pay you if your own debtor cannot or will not settle.

So if you can get one you will have two chances of being paid instead of one.

Guarantees are, however, only as good as the people or businesses giving them. If your guarantor has no money or assets you are going to be no better off.

To be enforceable a guarantee needs to be properly and legally drafted, so if you use one make sure it is prepared by a solicitor who is experienced in these matters.

Note

Sole traders and all the individual partners in a partnership are always fully liable for all the debts of their businesses and there is no need to secure a guarantee when trading with such firms.

Directors of limited companies are not personally liable for their companies' debts unless you get a guarantee from them.

Companies are liable to the full extent of their assets for any guarantees signed in their name.

Parent companies have no legal responsibilities to the creditors of their subsidiary companies unless they have signed guarantees to that effect.

A person who can't pay gets another person who can't pay to guarantee that he can pay.

Charles Dickens

Harassment

The Administration of Justice Act 1970 tells you what you can't do to recover your debts:

1. You can't harass your debtor with demands which, because of their frequency or manner, will cause him or his family alarm, distress or humiliation.
2. You can't falsely tell him that criminal proceedings will be taken as a result of non-payment.
3. You can't falsely represent yourself to him as being authorised in some official capacity to enforce payment of the debt.
4. You can't use documents which are falsely represented as official documents when they are not.

So be careful and be reasonable. Being too aggressive can land you in trouble–and still not get you paid.

What is exhilarating in bad taste is the pleasure of giving offence.
Charles Baudelaire

Inflation

If you extend £100,000 of credit for a period of one year and during that year the inflation rate averages 10 per cent per annum, you will have effectively lost £10,000 even if you are paid in full and right on time.

The reason for this is that the money you receive back at the end of the year will not go as far or buy as much as it did 12 months earlier. In fact, it will buy 10 per cent less or only 90 per cent of what it would have when you originally made the money available to your debtor.

Be constantly aware of how inflation discounts your accounts receivable. Allow for it in your costs of credit and in your profit margins. Take particular care when you are extending credit for long periods.

If our foresight was as good as our hindsight we would all be a damn sight better off.
Anonymous

Interest Charges on Late Payments

It is perfectly legal to charge a reasonable interest rate on your unpaid or late paid accounts.

If you think your goodwill will stand it and you want to do it, let your customer know your policy at or before the point of sale. If you do it afterwards it will not be enforceable.

If you decide you want to charge interest make sure the rate to be charged is clearly stated on your delivery dockets, invoices, statements, terms and conditions of sale, and any other relevant documents.

From a practical point of view the cost of administration can often make interest charging and collecting more of a minus than a plus. That is, unless the amounts involved are sufficiently large to make them worthwhile.

However, just the fact that you are able to insist on interest does give you some leverage when asking for your account to be paid.

Also, if your debtor is late in paying it can mean that he pays for financing his lateness instead of you.

He was always late on principle, his principle being that punctuality is the thief of time.

Oscar Wilde

Internal Information

This is the information available from your own eyes and ears.

It is also what your collection people, sales people, delivery people and the grapevine tell you or should tell you about your customers.

If you are owed or could be owed a considerable amount, or any amount, it is important for you to know that:

Your customer's staff level is about half what it was three months ago.
They have just closed three warehouses.
The MD has left and a new team has taken over.
The whisper around the trade is to watch out.
Your collectors are taking progressively longer and having increasing difficulty in getting paid.

So don't end up writing off a debt which you could have avoided by paying attention to the obvious right under your own nose—use the information that is available to you.

Don't talk about yourself, it will be done when you leave.

Addison Mizner

Invoices and Statements

Easily understood invoices and statements which are sent out as early as possible get better results than those that are unclear and late.

If you don't bill on time you can't expect to be paid on time.

It is a simple fact but one that is often overlooked in a busy day-to-day existence with so many other priorities demanding your time, but what can be more important than getting paid?

Similarly, your invoices and statements must tell your customer all he needs to know before paying them, because if they don't—he won't.

Send them to the right person at the right address for payment and include the following information:

1. What the debt is for and the date it was incurred. This should be in sufficient detail for precise identification.
2. The exact date by which the account must be paid. State clearly that the account is due no later than 7 July. Do not use terms like 'nett monthly'.
3. The amount of VAT involved, and your VAT number if you have one.
4. An account number or clear reference such as an order or delivery note number for identifying the invoice or statement.
5. The full name and address to which the account must be paid and also its telephone number complete with area code.

Note

1. If litigation is ever necessary it is vitally important to your chances of success that your invoices and statements are issued in the full and correct name of your customer. This should always be double checked when you issue the first invoice to a new customer.
2. Don't ever include an aged analysis on your customers' statements. It can and does encourage your customer to pay only the oldest parts of your total debt and leave the more recent balances unpaid.
3. Use the open item method and show all unpaid invoices individually on your statement rather than bringing forward a single unpaid and undetailed balance from last month. This makes the statement easier for your customer to understand and reconcile and will help you be paid faster, as well as saving a lot of time on queries.
4. Where warranted, take the opportunity of adding a payment reminder note to your statement. Even a handwritten note requesting

early payment of your account can get good results. It helps to make the message prominent by using red ink or something similar that catches the eye.

5. If you have a lot of one-off sales or sales involving a small number of invoices, consider combining your invoice and statement into one document. This will save a lot of duplication and will also help to speed up your cash flow. Just head it 'Invoice/Statement'.

6. If you are dealing with, and are dependent on, several big customers, it is worth finding out how and when they pay their debtors, and then fitting in with their procedures. It may mean changing your own procedures, but if it also means changing your bank balance for the better it may be well worth it.

Many credit problems are caused by the creditors not the debtors.
Debtors merely take advantage of a set-up they have been presented with.

Judging the Efficiency of Your Credit Control

There are lots of statistics you can use to judge the efficiency of your credit control.

The most regularly used is the 'DSO'. This stands for Days' Sales Outstanding.

It is simply a guide as to how long your customers take before paying their accounts.

It can be calculated with varying degrees of sophistication but the following will suit most businesses.

Assume the following figures:

Sales	
September	£32,000
October	£29,000
November	£31,000
December	£26,000
Debtors outstanding at 31 December	£72,000

To work out how many days' sales are represented by the total debtors outstanding at 31 December you proceed as follows:

		Number of days in sales month
Debtors at 31 December	£72,000	
Less December sales	£26,000	31
	£46,000	
Less November sales	£31,000	30
	£15,000	
Less October sales	£29,000	16
	(£14,000)	77

63

Debt Collection Made Easy

The number of days in October is worked out like this:

$$\frac{\text{Balance of debtors } \pounds15{,}000}{\text{October sales} \quad \pounds29{,}000} \times 30 \text{ days in October} = 16$$

Therefore at 31 December there were 77 days of sales not paid for, or in other words your DSO was 77.

If the next time your DSO is measured the number of days has increased, your collection results are getting worse. If it has gone down they are improving.

Note

If your DSO is around 77 days and your terms are 30 days you are not doing well. The national average for 30-day accounts is around 65 days. A more ideal and practical average would be around 40 days.

Actuaries are people who find accountancy too exciting.

Anonymous

Knowing When Not to Give Credit

Prevention is easier than cure.

If you give credit two things will happen: it will cost you money and give you problems.

Cash with order or cash on delivery is always better than cash some time in the future.

So if giving credit is more of a habit than a commercial necessity consider the following:

1. Does your competition give credit? Do they give it to everyone?
2. What does it cost you to give credit? Would you be better off lowering your prices and selling for cash only?
3. What effect would not giving credit have on your sales, your cash flow and your profits?
4. What should be the minimum size of order acceptable for credit?

The answers are:

Don't give credit unless you have to.

If you do give it, give it for as short a time as you can. When you have given it, do all you can to collect it as soon as it becomes due.

Note

It is always worth remembering that no man's credit is as good as his money.

It is an equal failing to trust everybody and to trust nobody.

Proverb

Law of Agency

The law of agency relates to situations where a person or a business legally commits another to an agreement by acting on their behalf as their agent.

When this happens and the authority of the person or business to commit the other is disputed, the law of agency decides the issue.

Fortunately the situation is quite clear.

When an agent makes a contract either the principal is liable or the agent is liable for a breach of authority. In the latter case the principal is not liable for the contract.

The bottom line for liability is that you are only legally committed to an agreement made by an agent when:

(a) You have authorised the agent to make the agreement on your behalf.

(b) It is the sort of agreement that the agent would normally make for you.

(c) It is the sort of agreement that you have let others know that your agent has the power to make on your behalf.

Only special notice from you to those involved that your agent's authority has ended will prevent you being liable once you have held out an agent as having the right to legally commit you to certain agreements.

My agent gets 10 per cent of everything I get, except my headaches.

Fred Allen

Liquidation

Whereas people go bankrupt, companies go into liquidation. They go into voluntary or compulsory liquidation.

Voluntary liquidation

There are two types:

1. A members' voluntary liquidation. The members are the company's shareholders.
2. A creditors' voluntary liquidation.

A members' voluntary liquidation usually happens because a company's shareholders want to close down the business and get their money back.

In such cases the company's directors must declare that their business is solvent and can pay all its debts within 12 months.

So if you are owed money by a company involved in a members' voluntary liquidation the chances that you will get all you are owed are good.

A creditors' voluntary liquidation usually happens because a company has to close down due to the fact that it can't pay its debts.

In such cases the company's directors pass a resolution that the company be wound up.

Shortly after that they must call a meeting of their creditors and present a statement of affairs including a list of all the company's debts.

At this meeting the creditors will be asked to endorse the resolution to wind up the company and to approve the choice of a liquidator.

The majority vote carries the resolution. The majority in this case means the majority in value. That is, the value of each vote is equal to the amount owed to the creditor casting that vote. In other words, the more you are owed the greater is the value of your vote and your influence.

Creditors may vote to accept or not to accept either the voluntary liquidation or liquidator. Also, any creditor may decide to lodge a court petition for the company to be compulsorily wound up.

Compulsory liquidation

If the court accepts the creditors' petition and grants a winding up order the company will come under the control of the Official Receiver (a civil servant from the Department of Trade and Industry known as the OR).

The first thing the company must then do is submit to the OR a full statement of its financial affairs as well as any other relevant information.

If the OR is not satisfied with this report he may recommend a detailed investigation into the reasons for the company's failure. In such cases the court will arrange for the appropriate enquiries to be made.

However, if the OR is satisfied the next step in the liquidation is for a meeting of creditors and shareholders to decide whether or not to appoint an outside liquidator. If an outside liquidator is not appointed the OR will continue as liquidator.

The liquidator's main task is then to sell the company's assets and distribute the proceeds to creditors under the court's supervision.

The proceeds are not, however, distributed on a pro rata basis. Various up-front creditors are not only paid first but, if the money is available, they are usually paid in full. The balance, if any, is then distributed to the remaining and less fortunate, unsecured creditors on the basis of so much in the pound.

These up-front creditors are usually the Inland Revenue (tax), HM Customs and Excise (VAT), unpaid employees and those with registered charges, usually the banks.

It is the supervision by the court that is the main difference between a compulsory winding up and voluntary winding up.

Notes

1. To register a claim on the liquidator's list, simply write to the company's registered office, which you can normally get from their letterhead.
2. If directors of a company accept credit when they know their company is insolvent they can be personally liable for the debts incurred. They can also be disqualified from acting as directors of companies in the future.

'Either he's dead or my watch has stopped.'

Groucho Marx

Litigation

If your debtor has money and no legitimate excuse for not paying what he owes you, the only solution may be to take him to court.

In England and Wales this will mean the County Court, unless your debt is over £5000 when it will mean the High Court.

In Scotland, Northern Ireland and the Channel Islands it will mean the local courts.

In the County Court you may file the necessary documents yourself, employ a solicitor or use a collection agency.

As you can see from the table on page 73 the methods of recovery are quite varied. So whoever handles your case must know what they are doing, otherwise they may not only cost you time and money but also any chances of ever collecting.

Regardless of whoever is handling the case you must be sure:

(a) That your debtor has the money to pay you. If not, you could be simply throwing good money after bad.

(b) That there is reasonable evidence to support your claim.

(c) That you have the full and correct name and address of your debtor (or debtors if there is more than one). This sounds basic but you would be surprised how many creditors don't know who their debtor really is in strict and precise legal terms.

(d) That your debt is not over six years old. If it is you cannot sue (there are exceptions to this but they are rare).

If you are sure of all these facts then you are ready to proceed.

The first thing is to decide which court you want to use. Generally you have two choices: where your debtor lives or carries on his business, or where the debt was incurred. Sometimes there can be other considerations such as where the cause of action arose, but these are the main two choices. Courts are listed in Yellow Pages under 'Courts'.

Having decided which is the most convenient, apply to that court for a summons to be issued against your debtor for the amount owing plus the cost of the summons.

Interest may also be added from the date the debt became due. The statutory interest rate is usually fixed around the average overdraft rate, but you may be able to charge more if you have a private arrangement for interest in your terms of sale. However, it is always open to the court to strike out an unusually high rate of interest if it considers it to be unfair.

The court then issues the summons and serves it on your debtor, usually by post. If for some reason the post is ineffective then there are provisions for other types of service.

Debt Collection Made Easy

The summons gives your debtor 14 days to pay or let the court know why he won't.

If he pays, that is the end of it.

If he explains to the court why the debt hasn't been paid, you and he will be given a date for the case to be heard.

A judge or registrar will then listen to both your stories and decide the case.

If he does nothing you may proceed to enter judgement.

Sometimes there are combinations and variations on the above, such as requests for part payments or for time to pay. In these cases the court will decide what is to be done.

If your claim is under £500 it will be heard in what is known as the small claims court and the hearing will be less formal.

However, let's assume you have got judgement. Judgement means that the court agrees that your debtor owes you the money as stated on the judgement which is normally your debt, the interest and some costs.

The next step is to ask the court to help you get that money. This is called *enforcement*.

There are six main ways to obtain it:

Warrant of execution

This involves a bailiff going to your debtor's home or workplace and seizing and selling sufficient of his goods to pay your debt and costs.

Attachment of earnings

This involves the court ordering your debtor's employer to make deductions from his earnings to pay you what is owed.

There is however a level below which your debtor's earnings are protected.

Garnishee proceedings

This involves the court ordering a third party who owes your debtor money to pay that money into court instead of to your debtor. It can also be applied to your debtor's bank account provided there is money in it. The court will then pass the money to you to pay the judgement debt.

Charging order

This involves registering a legal charge, like a mortgage, against any assets known to be owned by your debtor. You then request the court to order the sale of the assets so you can recover your debt.

Bankruptcy proceedings

This involves the obvious and is a great incentive for your debtor to discover that he really can pay you after all. It only applies to individuals.

Winding up proceedings

This is bankruptcy as applied to companies.

Finally, if enforcement is not working because no assets can be found, you can arrange for your debtor to attend court for an oral examination as to his financial situation.

This is done under oath and may reveal the whereabouts of previously secreted assets. Any lying by the debtor during the examination constitutes perjury, which is a serious and punishable offence.

If your debtor does not attend court as ordered the judge will repeat the order. If he fails to attend a second time the judge has power to commit him to prison for contempt of court.

This applies not only to individuals but to companies where the directors can be examined and to partnerships where the partners can be examined.

Oral examinations are intended to be a cross examination of the severest kind and your debtor will be required to bring his books, papers and documents into court with him. Although such examinations can be carried out by a court officer it is usually best to do it yourself and, indeed, some courts will even insist on this.

Note

Enforcement in theory is simple and straightforward. In reality there can be practical and technical problems which can make it difficult and sometimes impossible.

Always consider the economic practicalities of getting and enforcing judgement before starting litigation. It could save you a lot of wasted effort and money.

However, judgements are good for six years. So if your debtor has insufficient assets to pay you when judgement is given, all may not be lost. If his fortunes improve over the next six years you are still entitled to collect on your judgement debt.

The High Court

The High Court is also used for pursuing unpaid accounts provided they are over £600.

The drawback is that if your debt is under £3000 you can only recover your costs on the County Court scale and the difference in scale can make it an expensive exercise.

If your claim is £650 or less no costs at all will be awarded to you.

Advantages of using the High Court are:

1. It generally has more impact on debtors and moves along faster than the County Court.
2. It makes it harder for debtors to make offers and to delay proceedings.
3. The private enterprise sheriffs used by the High Court are paid on results and are considered to be more efficient than the public servant County Court bailiffs who get their salaries regardless of results.
4. Where your debtor has no assets in this country but plenty abroad, a High Court judgement can probably be enforced in the country where the goods are located. On the other hand, the enforcement of County Court judgements is currently restricted to England, Wales, Scotland and Northern Ireland.

Warning

These comments simplify a complex subject. They should be treated as a guide only and not as a complete or detailed study of the law.

If you go to Carey Street you will see a lot of people with long faces.
They are creditors. You may also see one man beautifully dressed, wearing
a gardenia in his buttonhole and smoking happily. He is a debtor.

Judge Geoffrey Howard

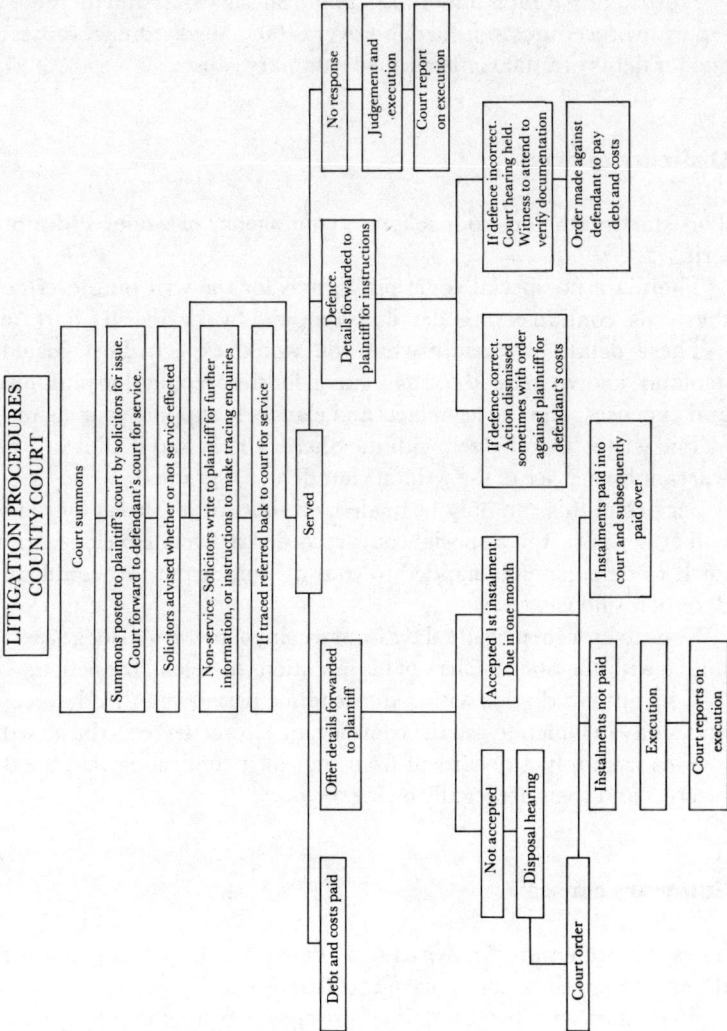

LITIGATION PROCEDURES COUNTY COURT

Court summons

Summons posted to plaintiff's court by solicitors for issue. Court forward to defendant's court for service.

Solicitors advised whether or not service effected

Non-service. Solicitors write to plaintiff for further information, or instructions to make tracing enquiries

If traced referred back to court for service

Served

No response → **Judgement and execution** → **Court report on execution**

Defence. Details forwarded to plaintiff for instructions

- If defence incorrect. Court hearing held. Witness to attend to verify documentation → Order made against defendant to pay debt and costs
- If defence correct. Action dismissed sometimes with order against plaintiff for defendant's costs

Debt and costs paid

Offer details forwarded to plaintiff

- Not accepted → Disposal hearing → Court order
- Accepted 1st instalment. Due in one month → Instalments paid into court and subsequently paid over
- Instalments not paid → Execution → Court reports on execution

Litigation—Scottish Style

Litigation procedures in Scotland differ from those in England but the course and the end results bear a general likeness.

Scottish litigation is undertaken in the Sheriff Court and there are two separate procedures: one for debts over £1000 called ordinary causes and one for debts of £1000 or less called summary causes.

Ordinary causes

This starts with you, your solicitor, your agency or whoever, drafting a writ.

There are no special court pro-formas for the writ but nevertheless they must contain certain details as required by the Sheriff Court Acts.

These details are really what you would expect. They include a demand, known in Scotland as a crave, for the amount due plus interest and expenses, and the legal facts and clauses to support your claim.

The writ is then lodged with the Sheriff Clerk, and if all is in order a warrant for service of the writ on your debtor is granted.

Service of this can only be made by a solicitor or Sheriff Officer who will either post it in a special court recorded delivery envelope, arrange for it to be personally handed to your debtor, or put through the front door of his house.

Your debtor then has 14 days from receipt of the writ to lodge a written notice with the Sheriff Clerk of his intentions to defend the action.

If he doesn't do this within the deadline period you then have a year and a day in which to ask the court for an extract decree to be issued.

This is simply a document from the court confirming that the debt, interest and costs are legally owing to you.

Summary causes

These are sometimes known as small debts and the procedures are quite different from those for debts of £1000 or more.

They start with the filling in of a pre-printed summons form which is obtained from the Sheriff Clerk.

A detailed statement of the claim is still required but in simpler and less formal terms.

Again, the summons is lodged with the Sheriff Court but from here on the proceedings are different.

The summons is returned to you, or whoever is acting for you, by the Sheriff clerk with two dates marked on it.

The first date is the return day. This is the day by which your debtor must return the reply form which is attached to the summons to the court.

The second date is the calling day. This is the day the case is called in open court. However, this only happens if your debtor wants to defend the action or makes you an offer which you can and do refuse.

On receipt of the returned summons you or your agent must now complete the service copy of the summons by putting in the return day and calling day and then arranging for it to be served on your debtor. Again, this needs to be done by either a solicitor or Sheriff Officer.

Once the service copy of the summons has been properly served the principal summons with details of the execution of service must be returned to the court before the return day.

The day after the return day you or your agents must check with the court to see if your debtor has returned his part of the summons.

If he has it will mean he either intends to defend the action or to admit the debt and make an offer to pay by instalments.

If the case is defended it is called in court on the calling day and you or your representative must appear or the case will be dismissed.

If instalments are offered, or your debtor doesn't return his section of the summons to the court, you or your agent must complete the minute book at the court no later than 24 hours before the calling date or your call will be dismissed.

At this stage the procedures are generally the same as for an ordinary cause and you have 366 days, or 367 days if it is a leap year, to ask the court for an extract decree to be issued.

Once you have your decree, be it for over or under £1000, you pass it to the Sheriff Officer for enforcement.

A Sheriff Officer is a person in private practice who has been appointed an officer of the court but is not a court employee.

Enforcement

The main methods of enforcement are as follows:

Poinding
This involves the Sheriff Officer going to your debtor's home or workplace and seizing sufficient of his goods to pay your debt and costs.

If the debt is still not paid 14 days after the goods are seized they can be sold.

Debt Collection Made Easy

Inhibitions

This action can be taken at the same time as your writ is issued and prior to judgement being given.

It is simply a method of inhibiting or stopping your debtor from cashing in his assets and putting them out of your reach before you have had a chance to recover what is owed to you.

Arrestments

You can arrest the bank account or salary of your debtor for the amount owing to you.

Also, if you know of a third party who is about to pay your debtor you can similarly arrest that money.

Arresting in this context simply means getting your hands on the money owed.

Insolvency

Finally, you can apply to have your debtor made bankrupt or, if a company, to be wound up if the amount you are owed is not paid to you.

Note

1. Enforcement in theory is simple. In reality it can be difficult and sometimes impossible.

   Always consider the economic practicalities before spending your time and money on taking your debtors to court.

2. An interesting sideline to Scottish litigation is how many English creditors don't take their Scottish debtors to court.

   The main reason for this is that they don't know how to and probably neither do a lot of their English solicitors.

   Naturally, either they or their solicitors can use a Scottish solicitor or agent to help them, but unless the debt is sizeable the tendency is to consider this too much time, trouble and expense.

   This is especially so if the case is defended, which can mean more time and money being spent on travelling to attend court.

   The same situation probably applies in reverse with Scottish creditors and English debtors, or indeed to any situation where debtors and creditors live in different legal systems.

Warning

These comments simplify a complex subject. They should be treated as a
guide only and not as a complete or detailed study of the law.

---

*Persons of good sense, I have since observed, seldom fall into disputation
except lawyers, university men and men of all sorts that have been bred at
Edinburgh.*

Benjamin Franklin

Making Them Pay—What Works

If your business is small you probably know from past experience what works and what doesn't in getting individual debtors to pay.

If your business is larger it takes more organisation and record keeping to know what the magic formula is for each customer.

Whatever the situation, it is important to your cash flow to be aware of just what works with each of your customers.

For instance, it is no good writing to a particular customer if historically he only pays after you have phoned him.

Similarly, why waste time and money phoning when the only way you have been able to get your money in the past has been to call in person.

Although most of us don't have the time or the inclination to record what tickles a particular customer's fancy when it comes to paying, it does nevertheless pay off to make that extra effort and note what it is that works—particularly with large customers.

Alas! How deeply painful is all payment.

Lord Byron

Minimum Credit Orders

These depend on your inclinations and your competition.

Regardless of these, orders below a certain value are hard to justify in terms of collection and administration costs.

The small money value of profits earned on minor sales can be so quickly absorbed by overheads that the whole exercise is hardly worthwhile.

The usual justification is goodwill and the hope that one day a small customer could become a large customer.

The counter-claim to this is that if your goods and services are competitive future trade will not be lost because you have a reasonable and commonsense approach to limiting credit orders to a certain size.

There is nobody so irritating as somebody with less intelligence and more common sense than we have.

Don Herold

Monthly Credit—Variations on a Theme

Most businesses give monthly or 30-day terms—or so they think.

What this usually means is that payment is expected by the last day of the month following the month in which the invoice is issued. That is, an invoice issued on 15 January would be expected to be paid no later than 28 February.

What it does not mean, except with the more experienced businesses, is that the account is due in 30 days. To mean that an invoice issued on 15 June would have to be due no later than 15 July. That is 30 days.

To join the more experienced businesses simply state your terms as being one calendar month from date of invoice, delivery, despatch or whatever is appropriate. That way, your 30 days terms will mean 30 days instead of meaning anything from 30 to 60 days (which averages out at 45 days or 50 per cent more days than 30 days).

Note

Whenever possible spell out your terms clearly with actual dates on all invoices and statements. Simply state 'due and payable not later than 15 July'.

Leave no room for misunderstandings of any type.

My life seems like one long obstacle course, with me as the chief obstacle.

Jack Parr

Moratoriums

When a business finds itself seriously short of cash it can often buy breathing time by approaching its creditors and asking for a moratorium on payments.

This is simply an agreement by each creditor to hold off and not to press his claim for settlement for an agreed period as long as the other creditors do likewise.

The reason creditors agree to such arrangements is to give their debtor time to sell assets, usually his stock, without the pressure of a forced sale and so realise a maximum rather than a minimum amount for the benefit of all involved.

Moratoriums are usually informal agreements, but if you are ever involved in one, make sure it includes plenty of protection clauses as well as a defined reporting procedure to ensure that you and the other creditors know what is going on and that you are all receiving fair treatment.

It is not death, but dying, which is terrible.

Henry Fielding

Not at Address Shown

If your mail to a debtor is returned with this notation and he has forgotten to leave you his new address all is not lost.

Simply write to the people or the business next door and ask if they know your customer's new address. You will not always get a reply but you may be surprised at how often you do. You may also be surprised at how often they say he is still there!

Just address your enquiry to:

The Occupier
4 St George's Street
Manchester M1 5QP

Failing that there are a large number of firms throughout the country who specialise in finding missing debtors.

So unless your customer is particularly devious, and is good at it, the chances are that he can be found quite quickly and for a reasonable fee.

For help just refer to Yellow Pages under 'Debt collectors', 'Tracing' or 'Detectives'.

Abscond. To 'move' in a mysterious way, commonly with the property of another.

Ambrose Bierce

Overseas Business and Export Credit

The business of export credit deserves a book of its own and many good ones are available.

What they all tell you is that doing business and controlling credit overseas is much the same as it is at home except that it is more complicated and expensive.

The problem is that you are dealing with foreigners who insist on having different money, customs, languages, politics, legislation and living a long way away.

All these factors must be allowed for, particularly in your profit margins.

Questions for exporters include:

1. Where are you going to export, to whom, and is his credit any good?
2. Who will you use to check out his credit—local bankers, your own bankers, your credit insurance underwriters, local import agents, credit agencies or trade references?
3. How is he going to pay you?
   (a) **By cash in advance.**
   (b) **By open account with payment due so many days after receipt, after delivery to the docks or some other criteria.**
   (c) **By letter of credit.** This is where your purchaser makes arrangements at his bank to pay you at your bank subject to certain pre-agreed conditions being met.

   Letters of credit can be confirmed, which means the money is guaranteed by a bank in your country, or unconfirmed, which means it isn't. Confirmed is better, but make sure the bank doing the confirming is a reputable one.
   (d) **By bill of exchange or promissory note.**
   (e) **By a factoring company.**
   (f) **By forfaiting.** This means you get the debt guaranteed by a bank in the buyer's country, then sell it at a discount to another bank.
   (g) **By countertrading.** This involves you or someone else in a chain with you being paid by goods, services or benefits, instead of in real money.
4. Are you going to insure your debts?

   If so are you going to use one of the commercial companies or do it through the government-backed Export Credits Guarantee Department?

5. How, if at all, are you going to protect yourself against changes in the exchange rate between your currency and your customer's currency?

   Are you going to sell your customer's foreign currency forward, take out a currency loan or cover it some other way?

   Selling forward means selling the foreign currency today for delivery at the time you expect to receive it from your customer.

   The price you are quoted today reflects the current exchange rate for the foreign currency adjusted for interest for the period until delivery.

   Taking out a currency loan means borrowing the invoice value in your customer's currency, converting it to your own currency, and then repaying the loan when your customer pays you.

   Using either of these two methods you know exactly what you are receiving in your own currency and can adjust your price accordingly.

6. How are you going to make sure your customer's payment to you won't be stopped by his government's policies, which is always possible where there are balance of payments or political problems?

   Are you going to use credit insurance, take your chances, use some of the methods already described or cover yourself by some other method?

7. What are you going to do if your customer won't pay you? Are you going to use your local agents or staff, a debt collector, a solicitor, political pressure or what?

Other questions are almost endless.

A good starting point for help, if you don't already have connections in this field, is your bank, who will refer you to one of their specialist export departments or to one of the official export agencies. Larger exporters will probably need more specialised advice.

Foreigners—Who's 'im Bill? A stranger!
'Eave 'arf a brick at 'im.

Punch

Part Payments

Part payment is better than no payment.

However, if you are not satisfied with being put off with less than your full due, simply adjust the balance outstanding and continue exactly as before with your collection procedures.

On the other hand, if you feel your debtor is making a reasonable effort to reduce his debt, then enter into an agreement with him for the payment of the remaining balance.

If he then varies or strays from the agreement in an unsatisfactory way you are only asking for trouble if you don't act promptly for full recovery.

Also, while he is paying and after he has paid, don't add to your worries by giving him more credit.

If you do the chances are good that you will only have the same situation all over again or probably even worse.

If you give a man more than he can do he will do it.
If you only give him what he can do, he'll do nothing.

Rudyard Kipling

Post-dated Cheques

From time to time, hard-pressed debtors will offer you post-dated cheques.

If you are definitely not going to get anything else take them—but negotiate the shortest terms you can.

The advantages of post-dated cheques are:

1. They are better than no cheques.
2. They might be paid on presentation.
3. If they are not paid on presentation they do represent proof of your debt and are good evidence if litigation is necessary.

If your post-dated cheque does bounce don't hesitate. Demand a banker's draft or real cash by return mail or personal delivery and then, if this is not received don't hesitate, commence immediate legal proceedings.

If you do waste time the chances are good that your debtor will go under and you will get nothing.

We must use time as a tool, not as a couch.

John F Kennedy

Price Loading to Cover Financing

If you know in advance that a customer is going to take six months to pay you instead of one and you still want to make the sale, then consider loading your price to cover your finance costs.

Explain to your customer that if your price is paid now or in one month that is one thing, but if it is paid in six months or more then that is another, that other thing being your costs of financing which come straight off your profit margin.

If you can agree a finance adjusted price then you can make your sale while still maintaining your profit margin, and your customer can get the extended credit terms that he wants and presumably needs.

Alternatively, finance for the sale may be available from a third party such as a bank, finance house, hire purchase or leasing company.

Either way you can make a sale to a customer who otherwise may not be able to buy from you or who you may not have previously considered as a prospect.

Note

Don't forget the effect of such sales on your cash flow and liquidity.
Also don't forget to consider why he can't pay you until later.

What you see is what you get.

Anonymous

Promissory Notes and Bills of Exchange

Both can be used as a way of paying debts and both have their advantages.

A promissory note is like a post-dated cheque. It is a written promise by your debtor to pay you a certain amount on a certain date.

Its advantages are:

1. It is a specific and unconditional agreement to make a payment of a fixed amount on an agreed date.
2. It is clear proof from your debtor that the amount stated on the note is correct and that the due date is undisputed.
3. It is a written promise, which is better than a verbal one.
4. It is negotiable, and if the drawer is of financial substance or if it is supported by some sort of security, cash may be raised by discounting it, selling it, or lodging it as collateral for a loan.
5. Many customers would have few qualms about late paying but would be reluctant to dishonour a promissory note which would come to the attention of their bank manager.

A bill of exchange, instead of being made out by your debtor, is made out by you then signed as 'accepted' by your debtor.

Promissory notes and bills of exchange are often guaranteed or endorsed by a third party of financial standing. This makes them even better because if there is a problem you will have two chances of being paid instead of one.

Although these methods of payment are not usual for normal trade credit transactions they should be considered where sizeable amounts or longer than normal credit terms are involved.

Half the promises people say were never kept, were never made.

Ed Howe

Queries and Disputes

Queries and disputes provide the greatest excuses ever for not paying accounts.

To get paid you must resolve them quickly.

If they can't be resolved then agree on the amount of the problem involved, isolate it and ask for the payment of any uncontested balance.

If your customer is genuine he should respond positively to this fair approach. If he doesn't you stand warned of the type of person you are dealing with and should act accordingly.

After isolating the problem, investigate it as quickly as possible, resolve it, make sure as well as you can that the system doesn't allow it to happen again, and proceed at full steam to collect whatever balance you and your custmer have agreed upon.

If you can't resolve the query or dispute with your customer then you really do have a problem and having a court decide for you may be the only solution. This, however, should only be a last resort.

He never wants anything but what's right and fair; only when you come to settle what's right and fair, it's everything that he wants and nothing that you want. And that's his idea of compromise.

Thomas Hughes

Reading Company Reports

Like computer people and bank managers, company directors have a language of their own.

When you read the reports of your debtor companies you may find the following of help in getting to what is really meant.

There has been a reduction in net profit margins.	We are in trouble and running at a loss or close to it.
We are suffering a mild cash flow problem.	They are about to cut off our phones, re-possess the furniture and lock us out of our offices.
In your board's considered opinion	Someone in the accounts department has had enough imagination to think up a plausible excuse for explaining the year's disastrous results.
Expansion and development plans are proceeding despite the difficult trading conditions.	The directors' new dining room and bar area will just about account for all this year's profit.
It is with deep regret we announce the resignation of	After years of infighting and back-stabbing one of the directors has finally had enough and is getting out.
Allowing for seasonal adjustments	We have managed to juggle the figures this year and let's hope we can make a real profit next year.
This year's directors' fees have been productivity linked.	Although profits have crashed the board has still managed to work out a way of giving itself a rise that is ahead of the rate of inflation.

Receivers

Generally, if security is given for a debt and default is made in repayment of that debt, the secured creditor is entitled to appoint a receiver to safeguard his interest.

The agreement pledging the security will usually have provision for the appointment. If not the receiver may be appointed by the court.

The receiver's job is to safeguard the creditor's security, and to sell sufficient of the charged assets to pay off the secured debt.

Once this has been done the receiver's job is finished and the remaining assets will revert to their owners or to less fortunate unsecured creditors.

So long as the receiver is in the driving seat neither the owners nor the unsecured creditors can do much to remove him. Nor can they do anything about his methods of selling the assets which have been charged. This applies even if he seems to be selling them too quickly or too cheaply.

It is not unusual for a receiver to continue to run a business while he is selling off the charged assets and in doing so to purchase goods on credit.

It is important in such circumstances to note that the receiver and not the business may be liable for any debts he incurs in this way.

If selling to a receiver you must be sure to establish whether the receiver is purchasing in his own name and assuming personal liability or whether he is purchasing on behalf of the receivership.

Either way you should make the normal credit enquiries to assure yourself you are dealing with someone or some business of substance. If not you could end up in receivership yourself.

In most cases receivership is followed by liquidation since the business is often left insolvent.

Receivers are also known as 'administrative receivers'.

It is probable that the Lord also loveth a cheerful loser.

Neville Hobson

Refusal of Credit

Occasionally someone may tell you that refusing credit can be the basis for legal action on the grounds that a reputation has been unfairly damaged by a refusal to give credit in a business where giving credit is normal.

This is not true.

No one is legally obliged to give credit if they don't want to.

Naturally, you cannot say you are not giving credit because you think the applicant is not trustworthy. That could get you into trouble.

All you have to say is 'no'. You don't have to explain why.

It is kindness to refuse immediately what you intend to deny.
Publilius Syrus

Retention of Title

Legal title to goods normally passes when they are received by your customer. He gets the goods and you get a debt owing to you.

However, if you include retention of title clauses in your conditions of sale you may be able to stop title passing until the amount owing for the goods is paid to you.

Retention of title clauses include provisions such as:

1. That you as seller retain ownership of the goods until you are paid for them.
2. That your customer holds the goods for you as a bailee.
3. That your customer has a fiduciary responsibility to you in respect of any monies received from the sale of the goods.
4. That the goods involved be stored in such a way that they are clearly identifiable.

However, the practicalities aren't always that straightforward. This is especially so when your goods have been changed into or mixed with something else or when your customer or your goods or both have disappeared.

Similarly, the legalities of enforcement are not always as straightforward as you may wish.

Nevertheless in most cases the right of possession and the right to the proceeds of the sale of your goods can only be helpful.

If you think it worthwhile for your business use a good solicitor to have your clauses drafted, advise your customers of your intentions and try it.

Don't, however, view the clauses as a watertight insurance policy because that they are not.

It is preoccupation with possession, more than anything else,
that prevents men from living freely and nobly.

Bertrand Russell

Sales Ledger

This is more than just a book with balances. Properly set up and organised it can tell you a great deal about your business and in particular your customers.

It can tell you:

1. The weekly, monthly and yearly volume of sales to each and every one of your customers;
2. What and when each customer has paid you and hasn't paid you;
3. What each customer's credit limit is, if he has exceeded it, and by how much;
4. The name of the sales person who made each sale;
5. The geographical area where each sale was made;
6. The full details and particulars of all goods or sevices sold;
7. The amount of all monies received and all monies owing.

Analysed, considered and acted upon these facts and the others also available from your sales ledger can go a long way towards helping you make your business more efficient and profitable.

Turnover is vanity.
Profit is sanity.

Here is what a sales ledger looks like:

Client: Unity Traders Ltd.
Address: 212 Cherry Lane
London NW1A 7BU
Contact: Mr J Smart
Managing Director
Telephone no: 01-789 1254

Terms: Accounts due for payment
at end of month following the date of invoice

Credit limit: Balance not to exceed £2500

Note: Refer any new order to Credit Manager if it will
cause the outstanding balance to exceed the credit limit

Invoice date	Invoice no	Due date	Details of purchase	Debit £	Credit £	Balance £	Sales representative
11.6.XX	1234	31.7.XX	10 Tyres (ref A342)	850		850	JR
28.6.XX	9876	31.7.XX	6 Aerials (ref L4781)	175		1025	JR
15.7.XX	0023	30.8.XX	5 Radios (ref E113)	210		1235	PM
12.8.XX			Cheque		1025	210	

Sales v Credit

Sales people often view the credit department as an obstacle to overcome in getting a sale.

Credit people often view the sales department as an obstacle to overcome in getting a profit.

Comments by sales about credit are usually along the following lines:

1. By the time they approve credit the sale has gone to someone else.
2. They keep losing good business by not wanting to give credit or by wanting to give too little.
3. They keep upsetting customers by pushing them for money.
4. They constantly expect us to get involved in sorting out their problems.
5. They are not flexible enough.

Comments by credit about sales are usually along the following lines:

1. They don't do their paperwork properly and then expect an answer this afternoon.
2. They want to increase sales by selling to anyone regardless of whether we are likely to get paid or not.
3. They make it hard for us to collect by telling our customers not to worry too much about our terms of payment.
4. They give wrong information and then they don't want to know about any queries or problems.
5. They keep wanting to supply goods without going through the proper procedures.

Getting these two sets of very different people to work for a common cause isn't always easy but, as well as you can, make sure both understand that:

(a) The name of the game is not just big orders but big orders that pay on time.
(b) To provide service and to compete for sales, paper work and credit decisions must be processed as quickly as possible.
(c) Getting the paper work right the first time saves the customer being bothered with further questions.
(d) Bad debts and slow paying accounts don't help to pay high salaries and bonuses.
(e) To get the best out of the situation both sides must try to understand how the other man goes about his work, what his

problems are and how you can best communicate with him to your own advantage.

Men are never so good or so bad as their opinions.
Sir James Macintosh

Solicitors

Solicitors handling debt collecting and documentation for credit control are like the rest of society. They range from excellent to good to bad to worse.

Their inclination in regard to fee charging follows a similar pattern.

For best results it is advisable to find a specialist in what you want rather than one whose main business is divorces, conveyancing or racehorses.

So-called all-rounders are also best avoided.

Solicitors are a society of men bred up from their youth in the art of proving by words, multiplied for the purpose, that white is black and black is white according as they are paid.

Jonathan Swift

Standing Orders and Direct Debits

Unfortunately, these are not a practical or acceptable means of collecting debts in most industries.

Also they won't help if your debtor is short of cash—either his bank won't pay or he'll cancel them.

But if you can use them they will certainly overcome many of the built-in delays involved in getting your bills paid on time.

They are particularly good where regular weekly, monthly, or yearly payments ae due, as they are for cleaning, garaging, insurance and so on.

They are also helpful if they are arranged so that you are paid on or before the date of delivery of your goods or services as compared with the usual 40- to 70-day wait for your cheque.

These methods of payment are more likely to be accepted if they are requested right up front before you start to do business and if they are presented as being the only way you do business. Afterwards they are more difficult to get.

The direct debit is the more flexible to use of the two because the amount can be adjusted for VAT or other changes.

With standing orders the amounts involved are stated in advance and any change will mean a new standing order.

On the other hand, standing orders are cheaper to operate as your customer pays the bank charges whereas with direct debits you pay them yourself.

If it were done, when 'tis done, then 'twere well it were done quickly.
William Shakespeare

Status and Credit Reports

Information concerning a customer's ability to pay is important to any business.

The cost of the information must, however, be relevant to the size of the debt. There is no sense spending £10 to check on a £20 debtor.

All information available is necessarily historical but as the past is mainly a reliable guide for the future it is useful in helping you decide whether you should or shouldn't give credit.

The format for the many specialist companies supplying credit information on individuals and companes varies but the following sample reports will give you a broad idea of what's available.

Sample status report—individual

TO: Average Corporation Limited
125 High Street
LONDON NW1

Date: 12.4.XX

Your Ref: J Smith
Our Ref: MM/LL
Credit Proposed: £150 per month

INFORMATION REGISTERED SUMMARY

Subject: J Jones

Address given: 86 New Street
London SW7

County Court Judgements:		
	04.07.84	£1,429
	02.02.85	£43 (paid April 1985)
	15.08.85	£234
	06.09.85	£2,676

Insolvency Information: Bankruptcy Administration Order
dated 11.11.85
Adjudicated Bankrupt 14.02.86

Known Trade Payment Defaults:		
	02.04.84	£586
	12.12.84	£753
	06.06.85	£129
	04.11.85	£251

Known Financial Commitments: Fixed Term Agreement August 1984 for 24
payments of £86.60

Other Credit Information: Subject is registered on electoral roll as residing at
address given with Sally Anne Jones and Fred
Jones

Comments: As the subject has been adjudicated bankrupt credit transactions
cannot be recommended.

Note. All information in this report is provided in confidence

Sample credit report—company

TO: Average Corporation Limited   Date: 01.11.XX
      125 High Street
      LONDON NW1   Your Ref: J Smith
                                         Our Ref: MM/LL
                            Credit Proposed: £1000

INFORMATION REGISTERED SUMMARY

Company Name: Jones Power Tools Limited
Previous Name: The Electrical Machine Company Limited (changed 12.04.82)
Registered Office: 100 New Road, London SW7
Registered Number: 123456
Date of Incorporation: 03.04.80
Directors: H R Jones   B J Walker   L Howard-Smith
Company Secretary: C Walters
Issued Share Capital: As at 15 January 1987   £100
Major Shareholders: H R Jones   55%   B J Walker   45%
Principal Activities: Engineers specialising in power tools for the aviation industry

FINANCIAL SUMMARY for the year ending 15th January

Turnover		Pre Tax Profit	
1987	£183,231	1987	£7,143
1986	£310,932	1986	£28,548

After Tax Profit
1987	(£2,521) loss
1986	£9,127

Shareholders Funds (including Paid Capital)
1987	(£6,211) deficit
1986	£7,458

Working Capital
1987	(£16,348) deficit
1986	£3,418

County Court Judgements:	July 1984	£542
	June 1985	£345 paid October 1982

February 1986   £1,795
April 1986   £986
January 1987   £2,421

Insolvency Information: Petition filed August 1987
Liquidator appointed September 1987

Known Trade Payment Defaults:

	April 5	£586
	December 1985	£753 (Paid)
	June 1986	£129
	July 1986	£1,203
	February 1987	£1,974
	June 1987	£524

Registered Charges: There is a registered charge over the company's total assets
for all monies due to Natlay Bank

Known Financial Commitments: Fixed term agreement from August 1984 for 48
payments of £152

Comments: As the company is now being voluntarily wound up credit dealings
can not be recommended

---

*He uses statistics as a drunken man uses lamp-posts — for support rather
than illumination.*

Andrew Lang

Stickers

These are the adhesive labels stuck on to invoices and statements in the hope of encouraging debtors to pay you.

They come in all sizes, designs and colours and are available from stationers, specialist suppliers and some debt collecting agencies.

Evidence that they achieve any results other than taking up time and leaving you sticky is not, to the best of my knowledge, available.

At the end of the day you are either a sticker person or not a sticker person.

When a man comes to me for advice, I find out the kind of advice he wants, and I give it to him.

Josh Billings

Stopping Supplies

The threat of or the actual stopping of supplies or services can often produce payments when all else has failed.

But it will only work if further orders are required and other suppliers are not readily available.

The decision lies between the possibility of losing future business by stopping supplies or of running the risk of a bad debt or a slow paying debt by not doing so.

If the decision is made to stop then the first step is to advise your customer's buyer of the situation promptly. There is no sense in doing this, however, unless there is an order in the pipeline. It will only cause a problem where none exists and provide an excuse for delaying payments on existing debts.

Important

Credit facilities should only be reinstated once you are reasonably sure there will be no more problems with getting paid. If you have reservations only accept orders on the basis of cash on delivery.

If you are a specialist supplier or have a monopoly type of business, consider your customer's ability to stay in business if you cut off his supplies. Sending your customers broke is of little help to anyone.

It is easy to dodge our responsibilities but we cannot dodge the consequences of dodging our responsibilities.

Lord Stamp

Terms and Conditions of Sale

Every sale is a contract.

If you sell on credit your credit terms are part of that contract.

To protect yourself it is important that your conditions of sale and your terms of credit are known and agreed to by your customer at or prior to the point of sale.

To do this and to avoid the risk of future misunderstandings, ideally your terms and conditions should be:

In written form in straightforward language;

Precise and not ambiguous;

Signed and dated by your customer, who should receive a copy;

Fully discussed with and explained to your customer in advance to ensure they are clearly and fully understood;

Prominently stated on all estimates, delivery notes, invoices, statements and other relevant documents.

If your credit terms are 30 days or one month make sure your customer knows exactly what this means.

Does it mean:

1. One month from despatch;
2. One month from delivery;
3. One month from the invoice date;
4. One month from the end of the month when the goods or services were delivered or despatched;
5. One month from the end of the month during which the invoice was issued; or
6. One month from something else?

Other matters that should also be covered in your terms and conditions of sale are terms of delivery, details of warranties and guarantees and the conditions under which goods may be returned or credit notes issued.

Specimen contracts are available from the Institute of Purchasing and Supply and you can get further tips from your own suppliers' contracts or those of your competitors.

Creditors have better memories than debtors.

Benjamin Franklin

Time and Value Risks

Two aspects to be considered when assessing the risks of giving credit are how much and how long.

Giving £10,000 credit for one month is always riskier than giving £5000 credit for one month.

But giving £10,000 credit for one month can be less risky than giving £5000 of credit for six months.

The reason for this is that the sooner you can pursue your debts the greater will be your chances of recovery.

For instance, if one of your customers is in financial trouble and he owes you money which is due in 20 days, you are much better off than if the debt does not fall due for 100 days.

You can take action 80 days sooner and before the situation has had too much chance to worsen. Being able to do this may be the only factor standing between you and a bad debt.

Giving credit for extended periods is always more risky than giving it for shorter periods. If it seems necessary to give it over a long period make sure you fully consider your risk before proceeding.

All generalisations are dangerous, even this one.
Alexandre Dumas

Trade References—by Phone

It is easy to be cynical and think that new prospective customers will only give you their favourite trade references; which are just the ones you don't want.

However, you may be surprised at just how much you can find out from these references if you approach them with an open mind.

To do this the phone is recommended rather than the post. It's faster, more revealing, gives you a feel for the person you are talking to and the chance to encourage off-the-record remarks. Questions along the following lines are helpful:

How long have they been in business?
How long have you been in business?
Do they always pay on time or are they like everyone else?
How much business have you done with them over the last year?
When did you last deal with them?
Have there ever been any arguments or disputes with them?
Is it true their MD is your boss's brother-in-law?

Also don't forget the references they didn't give you.

It is usually not too difficult to look around and discover who some of their other suppliers are and to check with them as well if you consider this appropriate.

Also, if one doesn't already exist it may be possible to develop a credit information exchange in your industry or area where interested parties can share credit experiences for the common good. This is often done through an independent third party, such as a debt collecting agency, to ensure confidentiality.

We are inclined to believe those whom we do not know because they have never deceived us.

Dr Samuel Johnson

Trade References–by Post

More information can usually be gained by phone than by post. However, if circumstances dictate using the post then make the best of it by:

1. Sending a typed letter, or at least one that looks as though it is typed, so it looks personalised.
2. Writing to a named person. Normally the Managing Director is best. Get his name from your customer or phone the reference and ask for it. If you don't have time then simply write to the Managing Director.
3. Not asking too many questions. This can deter your reference from answering.
4. Using a simple and easy-to-answer format with all queries being as short and as telling as possible.
5. Enclosing a pre-paid envelope for the return of the answers.

A sample letter is as follows:

J Hardy Esq
Credit Manager
Flint Federated Limited
22 South Street
LONDON EC1B 4UP

Dear Mr Hardy

Brite Trading Limited, 12 Jones Street, London W1

Our above customer has given your name as a trade reference.

So that we may process their credit application could you please help us by answering the questions below and returning this letter in the enclosed envelope.

Naturally all comments will be confidential.

Your assistance in this matter will be much appreciated.

Yours sincerely

P Lindsay
Credit Manager

1. How long have they been credit customers? ....
2. What credit terms do you give them? ....
3. Approximately how much credit business have they done with you over the last year ....
4. When did you last deal with them? ....
5. Have you ever had any arguments or disputes with them? ....
6. How would you rate them as payers–good, fair or bad? ....

Twenty-one Day Notice

Under section 518 of the Companies Act 1985 if you are owed £750 or more by a company and it is overdue you can serve that company with a notice requesting payment within 21 days. This notice is known as a Statutory Demand.

If your account is not paid within the 21 days you may present a petition to the High Court, or in some cases to County Court, for that company to be wound up.

It is important that, if you take this course of action, you have definite evidence that an undisputed debt does exist and that all reasonable efforts have been made to recover it. If not, costs, which in the High Court can be substantial, may be awarded against you.

The main reason for using a Statutory Demand is not to drive your debtor into insolvency, which helps no one, but rather to bring pressure to bear on having accounts paid and having them paid quickly.

The advantage of a Statutory Demand over the filing of a High Court writ or County Court summons is that it tends to bring on matters at a faster and more urgent rate.

In skating over thin ice, our safety is our speed.

R W Emerson

Under-organised and Overworked

Too often too many of those responsible for credit control are not trained or organised for what they are doing. On top of that many of them necessarily have to divide their time to allow for the other tasks for which they are also responsible.

But with most businesses having something like 40 per cent of their current assets and around 25 per cent of their total assets tied up in monies owing from trade debtors (ie, the ones that can be converted into cash to pay their bills and wages) this is far from ideal.

It would seem only sensible that the person who is in charge of 25 per cent of your assets and is responsible to a large degree for the liquidity of your business is given a reasonable chance to do his job properly and is the best that you can afford. If he isn't you may run the risk of not being able to afford anyone!

Lots of people confuse bad management with destiny.
F McKinney Hubbard

Unpaid Accounts— the Hidden Expenses

When your customers don't pay you, you are the one who pays—and your bills may be more than you think.

Here are just some of the expenses you pay, all of which affect your profits and your bank balance.

You pay for procedural costs which include postage, telephoning, the preparation of duplicate invoices and further statements, the writing of letters, the arranging of standard follow-ups and for all the other internal procedures necessary when you are not paid.

You pay for people's time, including managers' time, credit department's time, typists' time, administrative staff's time, sales representatives' time, as well as having to contribute your own time as well.

You pay outside people to help you, such as debt collectors, tracing agents and solicitors, and you may even have to pay court costs.

You pay the financing costs for all those people who are your customers and who owe you money.

On top of all this, you have the less obvious costs incurred by the denial of the use of your funds that are tied up in outstanding debts.

This is money you would probably use to reinvest in your business by way of increased stock, new equipment or property. You might also use it to reduce your overdraft, to achieve discounts for early payment or simply to enjoy for your personal requirements.

So the sooner your unpaid accounts are paid, the sooner *you* stop paying and the greater are your profits.

The great requisite for the prosperous management of ordinary business is want of imagination.

William Hazlitt

Value Added Tax on Bad Debts

Generally, VAT cannot be waived on bad debts and you must pay the revenue even though you haven't been paid yourself.

However, if your customer has become officially insolvent you may be allowed to claim a refund of the VAT charged.

If in doubt as to how and when, check with your accountant or local VAT office.

The age of chivalry is gone. That of sophisters, economists and calculators has succeeded: and the glory of Europe is extinguished for ever.

Edmund Burke

What is Trade Credit?

Trade credit is an unsecured loan given to someone so they can use it to buy your goods and services.

Recovering it afterwards can also be similar to collecting an unsecured loan.

Trade credit properly controlled can increase both your sales and your profits.

Improperly controlled it can put you in the finance business and out of the profit business.

It is important to remember that the reason for letting your customers buy now and pay later is not to make a sale, but to make a profit.

The word credit comes from the latin 'credere' which means to trust.
No doubt it is meant in the same context as trust everyone but first shuffle the cards.
Peter Buckland

Who is Your Debtor?

To collect efficiently from your debtor you should have full information on who they legally are—especially if you ever need to take them to court.

As a minimum you should know whether your customer is an individual, a partnership, an incorporated company or something else.

For individuals you need to know their surname, a first name or initial and their sex.

For partnerships you need to know the same information as you need for an individual but for all partners.

For companies you need their full name, country of registration and registration number.

For governments, councils, local authorities, charities, clubs and customers established under some other legal criteria you need their full name, any relevant reference or registration number, and details of how they are constituted.

Where a customer is operating under a trading name you need to know who owns the name and who is trading as that name.

It is only by not paying one's bills that one can hope to live in the memory of the commercial classes.

Oscar Wilde

Why Debtors Don't Pay

The reasons are many, but the main causes of your customers' cheques not being in the mail are:

1. They haven't got enough money to pay everyone or maybe even anyone.
2. They have got enough money but they like to keep it for as long as possible.
3. They would rather that you paid interest on your overdraft than that they paid interest on theirs.
4. They know time is money so they have a policy of buying it with yours and everyone else's.
5. Their administration is in chaos and they don't know who they owe or who owes them.
6. They are a massive bureaucracy and everything takes forever and sometimes longer.
7. They are too busy making money to worry about paying bills.
8. They have a dispute and are not in a hurry to resolve it and lose a perfectly good excuse for not paying.
9. They haven't received your invoice or statement because it wasn't sent or it was sent to the wrong address.
10. They received your invoice late because it was sent late and it won't now be paid until next month.
11. They are just plain difficult and like giving everyone a bad time.

I finally know what distinguishes man from other beasts: financial worries.
Jules Renard

Useful Addresses

The following addresses and telephone numbers relate to references in this book, information centres and helpful organisations for those involved in credit management.

The Association of British Factors Limited
Markbys Moore Avenue
London Wall
London EC2Y 5HE
01-638 4090

British Export Houses Association
16 Dartmouth Street
London SW1H 9BL
01-222 5419

Export Credits Guarantee Department
50 Ludgate Hill
London EC4 7AY
01-382 7000

Hire Purchase Information Ltd
Greencoat House
Francis Street
London SW1H 0BH
01-828 0851

Institute of Bankers
10 Lombard Street
London EC3V 9AS
01-623 3531

Institute of Credit Management
Easton House
Easton on the Hill
Stamford
Lincolnshire PE9 3NH
0780 56777

Institute of Directors
116 Pall Mall
London SW1Y 5ED
01-839 1233

Institute of Purchasing and Supply
Easton House
Easton on the Hill
Stamford
Lincolnshire PE9 3NZ
0780 56777

International Chamber of Commerce
Centre Point
103 New Oxford Street
London WC1A 1QB
01-240 5558

The Law Society
113 Chancery Lane
London WC2A 1PL
01-242 1222

London Chamber of Commerce
69 Cannon Street
London EC4N 5AB
01-248 4444

National Association of Unsecured Creditors
17 Southampton Place
London WC1A 2EH
01-404 5777

National Federation of Self-Employed and Small Businesses Ltd
St Annes Road West
Lytham St Annes
Lancashire FY8 1NY
0253 720911

Office of Fair Trading
Field House
Breams Buildings
London EC4A 1PR
01-242 2858

Registrar of Companies
Department of Commerce
43-47 Chichester Street
Belfast BT1 4PJ
0232 234488

Registrar of Companies
Companies House
Crown Way
Maindy
Cardiff CF4 3UZ
0222 388588

Registrar of Companies
102 George Street
Edinburgh EH2 3JD
031-225 5775

Registrar of Companies
Companies House
55-71 City Road
London EC1Y 1BB
01-253 9393

Scottish Office
Dover House
Whitehall
London SW1A 2AU
01-270 3000

Small Firms Service
(Department of Employment)
Ring the operator on 100 and ask for Freefone Enterprise; you will be put
in touch with your nearest office.

It's not what you know but who you know that counts.

Further Reading from Kogan Page

Be Your Own Company Secretary, A J Scrine, 1987

Business Rip-Offs and How to Avoid Them, Tony Attwood, 1987

Customer Service, Malcolm Peel, 1987

Essential Management Checklists, Jeffrey P Davidson, 1987

Export for the Small Business, Henry Deschampsneufs, 1984

Finance and Accounts for Managers, Desmond Goch, 1986

Financial Management for the Small Business: a Daily Telegraph Guide, Colin Barrow, 1984

Going for Growth: A Guide to Corporate Strategy, Michael K Lawson, 1987

A Handbook of Management Techniques, Michael Armstrong, 1986

How to Be a Better Manager, Michael Armstrong, 1983

Importing for the Small Business, Mag Morris, 1985

Law for the Small Business: a Daily Telegraph Guide, 5th edition, Patricia Clayton, 1987

The Practice of Successful Business Management, Kenneth Winckles, 1986

Raising Finance: the Guardian Guide for the Small Business, 2nd edition, Clive Woodcock, 1985

Successful Expansion for the Small Business: a Daily Telegraph Guide, M J Morris, 1984

Understand Your Accounts, A St J Price, 1986

Winning Strategies for Managing People, Robert Irwin and Rita Wolenik, 1986

Index

Index